Endorsements

"Every Christian who values the Holy Scriptures and who prizes the gospel of the grace of God in Christ should know about John Wycliffe. Steven Lawson has made Wycliffe's story—a story of courage, conviction, and gospel passion—accessible and engaging for Christians of all ages. It is a thrilling story, told by a man who exhibits the same gospel passion that animated Wycliffe. Read it, learn from it, and above all thank God for raising up John Wycliffe. Pray that He will again in these days raise up men of like conviction and passion."

—Rev. Dr. Ian Hamilton
Associate minister, Smithton Church
Inverness, Scotland

"For evangelicals, the Middle Ages are often unknown territory in which they think that the Holy Spirit was not active. But such an idea fails to remember Christ's promise to build His church, and the Holy Spirit was doing exactly that during the medieval era. This exciting new book by Dr. Steven Lawson powerfully shows how God the Holy Spirit was very much at work in the Middle Ages, and one great example is the remarkable ministry of John Wycliffe, who later generations very rightly called 'the Morning Star of the Reformation.' Wycliffe's love for and advocacy of the preeminence of the Holy Scriptures, though, was not simply a foreshadowing of one of the deepest convictions of the sixteenth-century Reformers. It needs to fire the hearts of God's people in these trying times. May this volume be a means to that end!"

—Dr. Michael A.G. Haykin
Chair and professor of church history
The Southern Baptist Theological Seminary

"It is very good to see a new biography of John Wycliffe. I very much commend it for being well researched and written in such a way as to captivate a popular audience. I hope it will go a long way towards rehabilitating Wycliffe (one of my heroes) in the evangelical mind."

—Dr. Nick Needham
Pastor, Inverness Reformed Baptist Church
Lecturer, Highland Theological College

"We all owe a debt to Wycliffe. He was a forerunner of the Reformation and a forerunner of English Bible translation, leaving a testimony of faithfulness and boldness. We also owe a debt to Dr. Steven Lawson for once again writing such an inspiring and compelling biography. May this book serve to give us all a greater appreciation for and a deeper love for the Word of God and the God of the Word."

—Dr. Stephen J. Nichols
President, Reformation Bible College
Chief academic officer, Ligonier Ministries

The Bible Convictions *of*

John Wycliffe

The Long Line of Godly Men Profiles

Series editor, Steven J. Lawson

A Long Line of Godly Men Profile

The Bible Convictions *of*

John Wycliffe

STEVEN J. LAWSON

LIGONIER MINISTRIES

The Bible Convictions of John Wycliffe
© 2021 by Steven J. Lawson

Published by Ligonier Ministries
421 Ligonier Court, Sanford, FL 32771
Ligonier.org

Printed in Crawfordsville, Indiana
LSC Communications
0000721

ISBN 978-1-64289-329-8 (Hardcover)
ISBN 978-1-64289-330-4 (ePub)
ISBN 978-1-64289-331-1 (Kindle)

Cover illustration: Steven Noble
Interior design and typeset: Katherine Lloyd, The DESK

Scripture quotations are taken from the New American Standard Bible® (NASB), Copyright © 1960, 1962, 1963, 1968, 1971, 1972, 1973, 1975, 1977, 1995 by The Lockman Foundation. Used by permission. www.Lockman.org

Library of Congress Control Number: 2021931085

To Dr. Michael Cosgrove

Faithful Servant,
Supportive Friend,
Devoted Student of God's Word

CONTENTS

A Long Line
of Godly Men

Down through the centuries, God has raised up an army of valiant Christians who have come from all walks of life—from the ivy-covered halls of elite schools to the dusty back rooms of tradesmen's shops. These leaders have been called from all corners of this world, from densely-populated cities to rural hamlets.

Despite these differences, each of these pivotal figures possessed one common feature—an unwavering allegiance to the Word of God. Likewise, these stalwarts of the faith held deep convictions about the God-exalting truths known as the doctrines of grace. Though they differed in secondary matters of theology, they stood shoulder to shoulder in embracing these biblical teachings that magnify the sovereign grace of God in salvation.

These truths of divine sovereignty emboldened these men

to rise up and advance the cause of Christ in their generation. These luminous individuals soared with wings like eagles above their times, as the doctrines of grace empowered them to serve God in their appointed hour of history.

This book is a part of A Long Line of Godly Men series, which highlights key figures in the perennial procession of these sovereign grace men. The purpose of this series is to explore how these seminal leaders used their gifts and ministries to further the work of Christ in their time. Because they were faithful followers of the Lord, their examples are worthy of emulation today.

This volume focuses upon the man who was the driving force behind the first translation of the Bible into the English language: John Wycliffe. From the lecture halls of Oxford to the throne room of the King of England, Wycliffe exercised immense influence. His opposition to the Roman Catholic Church fueled courage for generations to come. As the "Morning Star of the Reformation," Wycliffe paved the way for the Reformers after him. His passion for the common people to have access to Scripture drove his desire to undergo the work of translating the Latin Vulgate into a translation of the English Bible.

I want to thank the publishing team at Ligonier Ministries for their commitment to this A Long Line of Godly Men series. I remain thankful for the ongoing influence of my former professor and late friend, Dr. R.C. Sproul.

I am also indebted to the team at OnePassion Ministries,

who have undergirded my efforts to produce this manuscript. I am immensely grateful to Carissa Early for editing this book and to Brian Fairchild, who helped with invaluable research on Wycliffe. Without their skillful help, this book would not be in your hands.

I thank God for my wife Anne, who has made enormous sacrifices that have allowed me to study and write these pages. The last day will reveal the fruit of her support.

May the Lord use this book to embolden a new generation of believers to bring their witness for Jesus Christ to this world. Through these pages on Wycliffe, may you be strengthened to walk in a manner worthy of your calling. May this biography be used for the exaltation of Christ and the advance of His kingdom.

Soli Deo gloria!
—Steven J. Lawson
Dallas
September 2020

CHAPTER ONE

Bible Champion

It is an old and true saying, that nations sometimes know little about some of their greatest benefactors. If ever there was a man to whom this saying applies, it is John Wycliffe, the forerunner and first beginner of the Protestant Reformation in this country.[1]

—J.C. RYLE

Over a hundred years before the history-altering Reformation, the most influential Englishman of the day was John Wycliffe. As a renowned scholar, Wycliffe was mightily used by God to recover the very truths that would later ignite the fires of the Protestant movement. His Bible-saturated life prepared the path for the Reformation that would follow over a century later. Because of his commitment to Scripture, Wycliffe

---

1 J.C. Ryle, *Light from Old Times* (Edinburgh, Scotland: The Banner of Truth Trust, 2015), 1.

was emboldened to become the strongest voice in England for recapturing the gospel. He fearlessly affirmed the authority and sufficiency of the Bible at a time when the empty traditions of the Roman Catholic Church had taken precedence.

The fourteenth century was an especially dark time for the church. Religious superstitions and pagan beliefs had risen to dominate the church and suffocate its life. The light of the gospel had been dimmed. The torch of the truth was nearly extinguished. The gospel of God was buried under the debris of centuries of ruinous error. It was during this dismal time that this prominent English theologian named John Wycliffe stepped onto the stage of history.

At the height of his influence, Wycliffe was the most formidable individual who first initiated the translation of the Bible into the English language. He was the pioneering leader in England who confronted the false gospel of Rome that was so predominant throughout the land. Wycliffe was also the first visible leader in England to recover the purity of the message of saving grace in the preaching of God's Word. In all these crucial matters, Wycliffe was the primary forerunner, and the repercussions of his ministry are still being felt to this day.

A DAY OF EXTREME DARKNESS

Prior to the fourteenth century, there had been no exceptional evangelical leader of any large-scale impact in England. To this point, there certainly had been no pulpit ministry that had sent shockwaves through the nation. Certainly, there was no short-age of preachers among the priests, monks, and friars—but they were predominately blind leaders of the blind. The noted historian of preaching John Broadus acknowledges, "Before Wycliffe, we find little in English preaching that is particularly instructive."[2] As in the days of the prophets, there was a famine in the land for the hearing of the Word of the Lord (Amos 8:11). Consequently, the people were being "destroyed for lack of knowledge" (Hosea 4:6).

The religious scene in England was as pitch black as a star-less midnight. The gospel was submerged under an avalanche of spiritual ignorance, superstition, and immorality. Sermons were full to the brim—and overflowing—with myths, fables, and empty traditions. Spiritual authority was not founded on Scripture, but on quotes from the church fathers, church tra-dition, ecclesiastical councils, and the pope. From the pulpit to the pew, the church was filled with unconverted people who were held captive in chains of unbelief. In this bleak era, the blazing beacon of the true gospel was barely flickering.

John Foxe, author of *Foxe's Book of Martyrs*, described this dark hour: "Christianity was in a sad state. Although every-one knew the name of Christ, few if any understood His doctrine."[3] Foxe further portrayed the spiritual bankruptcy in England this way:

---

2 John Albert Broadus, *Lectures on the History of Preaching* (New York: A.C. Arm-strong and Son, 1902), 187.

3 John Foxe, *Foxe's Christian Martyrs of the World* (Uhrichsville, Ohio: Barbour and Co., 1985), 31–32.

The Church was solely concerned with outward ceremony and human traditions. People spent their entire lives heaping up one ceremony after another in hopes of salvation, not knowing it was theirs for the asking. Simple, uneducated people, who had no knowledge of Scripture, were content to know only what their pastors told them, and these pastors took care to only teach what came from Rome.[4]

This shadowy time of spiritual ignorance was a dismal period for the bride of Christ. But gospel light would soon be reignited.

Unrecognizable as Christianity

Nineteenth century author J.C. Ryle summarized this deplorable time in pre-Reformation England: "The likeness between the religion of this period and that of the apostolic age was so small, that if St. Paul had risen from the dead he would hardly have called it Christianity at all!"[5] Thick clouds continued to shroud the English-speaking people.

If the gospel was to be reclaimed and the church restored to her singular gaze upon Christ, many questions needed to be addressed: Does authority over the church rest with the pope

---

4   Ibid., 32.
5   John Charles Ryle, *Principles for Churchmen: A Manual of Positive Statements on Doubtful or Disputed Points* (London: William Hunt, 1884), 358.

and tradition? Or does it rest on the Scripture alone? How can sinful man be made right with holy God? In the providence of God, who would be the influential figure to address these critical issues? And what would be the means by which He would accomplish this mission?

In the gloom of this darkness, God was preparing a man to light the path back to the fountain of truth, and to challenge the purveyors of blinding error. In one of his tracts, Wycliffe declared, "God forbid that truth should be condemned by the church of Christ, because it sounds unpleasantly in the ear of the guilty or of the ignorant."[6] No corner of the church would be spared the illuminating power of Scripture, wielded by this Bible-saturated figure.

STEPPING OUT OF THE SHADOWS

To confront these vital issues, John Wycliffe, the leading English intellect of this hour, stepped to the forefront to change the course of history. Wycliffe was the most learned scholar of his day and a professor at Oxford University, the top school in Europe. There, in the esteemed halls of academia, Wycliffe studied and taught at the highest level of scholarship for almost forty years. Possessing a brilliant mind, silver tongue, and prolific pen, Wycliffe became the premier figure

---

6   Robert Vaughan, *The Tracts and Treatises of John De Wycliffe* (London: Blackburn and Pardon, 1845), xlii.

of his generation who would illuminate the path to recovering the gospel and reforming the true church.

Wycliffe's entrance into church history marked a new day for the church in English history. To be sure, his path was prepared in part by other men like Robert Grosseteste[7] and Thomas Bradwardine.[8] But Wycliffe was the first biblically sound, theologically grounded preacher with any noticeable spiritual power and extended influence upon the nation.

He was known as the shining "Morning Star of the Reformation." In the night sky, the morning star is the celestial body that shines brightest during the final hour of darkness immediately before the dawn. In like manner, Wycliffe's role was to resurrect the first glimmer of gospel truth that penetrated the spiritual darkness of the British Isle in the fourteenth century. History records Wycliffe was the initial bright light to appear in the dark days preceding the formal Protestant movement. He was the sturdy figure who brought biblical truth to the English-speaking world, creating a glorious ripple effect for the centuries that would follow.

BORN ON A SHEEP FARM

Around 1330, John Wycliffe was born into an English family that owned a sheep farm near Richmond in Yorkshire, two

---

7   See David Schley Schaff, "Robert Grosseteste," *The New Schaff-Herzog Encyclopedia of Religious Knowledge*, vol. 5 (Grand Rapids, Mich.: Baker, 1951), 84–85.

8   See J.H. Merle d'Aubigne, *The Reformation in England*, vol. 1 (Edinburgh, Scotland: Banner of Truth, 1994), 76.

hundred miles from London in northern England. Wycliffe most likely received his early education from the village priest. At sixteen, Wycliffe left home for Oxford, where he enrolled in Balliol College, its oldest college. Three years into his studies, the Black Death, one of the most devastating pandemics in human history, swept through Europe. Beginning in 1349, this plague killed one-third of Europe's population and left 25 million people dead.[9] The fatal disease spread to England, killing 30–50 percent in its wake in London alone.[10] At Oxford, this terrible epidemic suspended classes and interrupted Wycliffe's studies, forcing him to postpone his education until school resumed.

This confrontation with death led to Wycliffe's conversion to Christ. While the exact details of his saving encounter remain untold, it was nevertheless at this time that Wycliffe came to know Jesus Christ and follow Him. J.H. Merle d'Aubigné describes Wycliffe's conversion:

> This visitation of the Almighty sounded like the trumpet of the judgment day in the heart of Wycliffe. Alarmed at the thoughts of eternity, the young man—for he was then a mere youth—passed days and nights in his cell groaning and sighing, and calling upon God to show

---

9 John Frith, "History of the Great Plague, Part 1: The Three Great Pandemics," *Journal of Military and Veteran's Health* 20 no. 2, accessed February 5, 2021, https://jmvh.org/article/the-history-of-plague-part-1-the-three-great-pandemics/.

10 Sharon DeWitte, "Mortality Risk and Survival in the Aftermath of the Medieval Black Death," *PLOS ONE* 7 (May 2014), accessed February 5, 2021, https://journals.plos.org/plosone/article?id=10.1371/journal.pone.0096513.

him the path he ought to follow. He found it in the holy Scriptures, and resolved to make it known to others.[11]

BRILLIANCE AT OXFORD

When Oxford reopened, Wycliffe transferred to Merton College in Oxford, where he graduated in 1356 with a Bachelor of Arts degree. He then returned to Balliol College to resume further studies and became a teaching fellow and Master in the school. In 1361, Wycliffe was ordained to the priesthood and began preaching as the rector of the parish church in Fillingham. Immediately, his pulpit presence was marked by an exceptional ability to expound the Word of God. He then exchanged this pastorate for one in Ludgershall, Buckinghamshire, because it was closer to Oxford. During this time, Wycliffe received his Doctorate of Theology (1366) and Bachelor of Divinity (1369) at Oxford.

Wycliffe soon began his career as a professor at Queen's College, Oxford, where he gained a reputation as its most brilliant and popular teacher in theology and philosophy. Other professors attended his classes in order to be better educated. Wycliffe spent most of the rest of his life lecturing at this highly acclaimed institution, where he became regarded as the top theologian and philosopher in England. In this academic role, Wycliffe was respected as one of the greatest thinkers of his age. Many claimed he was second to none in European thought.

---

11 J.H. Merle d'Aubigne and S.M. Houghton, *The Reformation in England*, vol. 1 (Edinburgh, Scotland: Banner of Truth Trust, 2015), 64.

During this season, Wycliffe began to emerge as the foremost champion of the truth of Scripture. In his lectures, he stressed that the infallible Word of God was the highest authority and surest guide in all matters. He refused to cite the teachings of the church fathers, the findings of councils, and the decisions of popes as carrying greater authority than the Bible. His appeal was to the Scriptures alone. Further, he denounced ecclesiastical corruption in high places among the church leaders, stressing the singular importance of the written Word and grieving over the lack of biblical teaching in pulpits. For this strict adherence to Scripture, he became known as "The Evangelical Doctor."

STEPPING INTO NATIONAL PROMINENCE

Wycliffe was suddenly propelled into national prominence as his growing reputation captured the attention of the King of England, Edward III. Wycliffe had developed a doctrine he called "dominion," which emphasized God's sovereignty as the highest authority over the earth. He taught that God has assigned His authority over earthly property and worldly possessions to the secular government. For England, this stewardship was to the King and Parliament. At the same time, God has delegated His authority over spiritual matters to the church.

The exercise of this divinely-delegated dominion was conditional, Wycliffe argued, depending upon the faithful service of men to God. If spiritual leaders, such as the pope or bishops, failed to humble themselves before God and to live pure and godly lives, they forfeited their right to preside over church buildings and ecclesiastically-held land. In such cases, Wycliffe maintained that the state held the right to take possession of the church's holdings. The monarchy and nobility longed to claim the vast properties of the immensely wealthy English church. So this teaching was one they eagerly supported. This was at a time when the church owned a staggering one-third of the landmass of England.

APPOINTED BY THE KING

King Edward III supported Wycliffe's position of dominion, as he was paying a heavy price to fund England's war with France. Moreover, Pope Gregory XI in Rome had issued a burdensome tax upon the English government and church. Due to the king's senility, the real power behind the English throne at this time was the king's younger son, John of Gaunt, the Duke of Lancaster. The royal prince solicited Wycliffe's help to persuade Parliament that the king could refuse payment to the pope. He also asked for Wycliffe's aid in garnering much-needed resources from the church's properties in England.

Wycliffe successfully presented this argument to Parliament, which caused him to rise to such immense favor with the king that he was appointed a Royal Commissioner. In this position, he was sent to Bruges, France, to represent the English crown. He assisted in negotiations with a papal delegation concerning England's refusal to pay tribute to the pope. This authorization to represent King Edward III, the church in England, and the national interests of the country displayed the commanding respect Wycliffe had earned.

The appointment to represent England placed Wycliffe and his work in the context of a broader resistance to what is known as The Avignonese Captivity of the Papacy, in which a pseudo-papacy had been established in France under the control of the French government. Urban V, the ruling pope in Avignon, had demanded an overdue payment from England, further adding strength to the rising tide of political and ecclesiastical turmoil sweeping Europe. Dealing with such glaring corruption must have fueled Wycliffe's intense disdain for the papacy—French and Roman—that would mark his ministry for the rest of his life.[12]

PREACHER OF UNUSUAL POWER

When Wycliffe returned from France in 1374, the king appointed Wycliffe to be the rector of the parish church at Lutterworth, a small town near Rugby. This appointment placed Wycliffe closer to Oxford and his professorial duties in the classroom. He served in this pastorate for the next ten years until his death. This appointment opened up a new arena of ministry for Wycliffe, giving him a weekly pulpit in which to proclaim the truth of Scripture to a local congregation. After lecturing throughout the week at Oxford, he preached

---

12 J. Loserth, "John Wycliffe," *The New Schaff-Herzog Encyclopedia of Religious Knowledge*, vol. 12 (Grand Rapids, Mich.: Baker, 1951), 456.

on Sunday at Lutterworth. He also preached in other places around England, including London, as his gifts in preaching were visibly recognized by many. The people of England were hungry for rich spiritual meat. Wycliffe's teachings, rooted in the Bible and the exaltation of Christ, were unlike anything offered in England's present religious drought.

So noteworthy was Wycliffe's preaching that the King of England also made him a Royal Chaplain, granting him access to preach before the royal court. In this role, Wycliffe began publicly rebuking the pope's abuse of power, asserting that the Bible is the sole criterion for establishing any doctrine. No pope or ecclesiastical council, he argued, can add anything to the teaching of Scripture. Further, Wycliffe asserted that the authority of the pope has no basis in the Bible. At most, he insisted that the pope had authority over only one local church in Rome. At worst, he called the pope the antichrist. This latter claim caused Pope Gregory XI to vehemently respond by condemning Wycliffe as a heretic.

PAPAL BULLS FROM ROME

On May 22, 1377, the pope issued five papal bulls against Wycliffe, addressing nineteen theological errors from his writings. The professor-preacher was charged with being "the master of errors" and ordered to come to Rome for a formal examination and certain indictment for heresy charges.[13] But

13 The Pope to King Richard II.

Wycliffe refused to appear in Rome, reaffirming that the pope had no authority to summon him. Instead, Wycliffe appeared before the Archbishop at Lambeth Place, London. He began his *Protestatio* with: "I profess and claim to be by the grace of God a sound (that is, a true and orthodox) Christian and while there is breath in my body I will speak forth and defend the law of it. I am ready to defend my convictions even unto death. In these my conclusions I have followed the sacred Scriptures and the holy doctors, and if my conclusions can be proved to be opposed to the faith, willingly will I retract them."[14]

Because Wycliffe openly opposed the pope, he was quickly developing into the university's most controversial figure. So contentious was the heated confrontation created by this attack from Wycliffe that King Edward III and John of Gaunt were forced to distance themselves from him as his political protectors. At this point, the administrative leadership of Oxford was also forced to withdraw its support from their crowning scholar. In the eyes of the monarchy and the university, Wycliffe had gone too far in his assault upon the teaching of Rome. He had become too much of a liability. This reform-minded theologian, nevertheless, held his ground and refused to back down from his biblical convictions.

THE CONTROVERSY ESCALATES

Further escalating the controversy in which Wycliffe found

---

14   John Wycliffe, *Protestatio*.

himself was a heated time of civil unrest in England, marked by the Peasants' Revolt (1381). Wycliffe's teachings were unfairly blamed for having caused the turmoil, though he was not involved in this defiance against the government and even disapproved of it. But his opponents made strong accusations that this upheaval was the direct result of Wycliffe's supposedly radical teaching. The leaders of the church called for an investigation into Wycliffe's writings, resulting in the Blackfriars Synod. The powers-that-be met and formally condemned Wycliffe, bringing a further stigma upon his reputation. Where being a Wycliffite was once a popular badge to wear, it now indicated that one was a volatile threat to the peace of the nation.

Rather than backing down, Wycliffe responded courageously in the spring of 1381 by publishing a document known as *The Twelve Conclusions*, which targeted the jugular vein of the Catholic church—the Mass. This work was written one hundred thirty-six years before Luther would post his famous Ninety-Five Theses that protested the sale of indulgences. But Wycliffe's writing was equally groundbreaking in its heated attack upon Rome. In this document, Wycliffe condemned the belief that the real presence of Christ dwells in the bread and wine during the Eucharist.

BOLD BEYOND PRECEDENCE

Concerning Wycliffe's theses, John Laird Wilson wrote: "These theses were bold beyond precedent. Nothing so daring had been done in the entire history of the medieval church. The boldness of the attack can only be understood and appreciated, when it is borne in mind that the real presence was . . . regarded as the cardinal doctrine of the Church. It was the very center and citadel of the faith. The blow fell like a thunderbolt. . . . The Church was attacked at its very life center."[15]

Such a direct attack refuting the core doctrine of the Church from such a revered figure as Wycliffe demanded an immediate response from his opponents. The Chancellor of Oxford, William de Berton, declared *The Twelve Theses* to be not merely erroneous, but heretical. He pronounced that any public teaching of these statements was prohibited, including teaching from its most stalwart proponent, Wycliffe. Anyone discovered teaching these doctrines would be suspended, excommunicated from the church, and possibly even imprisoned.

FORCED DISMISSAL FROM OXFORD

Wycliffe stood firm. He continued to teach his convictions at Oxford, denouncing the transubstantiation taught in the Roman Catholic Church's Mass. One day, as Wycliffe was in his professor's chair in class, lecturing on the Lord's Supper, an officer of the university entered the classroom and abruptly issued Wycliffe a permanent dismissal from the university. Wycliffe was escorted from his class, never again to return to

---

15 John Laird Wilson, *John Wycliffe, Patriot and Reformer: "The Morningstar of the Reformation"* (New York: Funk & Wagnalls, 1884), 164.

his teaching duties at Oxford. The most popular professor at Oxford was now disgracefully removed from this esteemed platform, left to withdraw to his quiet pastorate in Lutterworth. The winds of worldly favor had shifted to howl against him. However, it would be in this secluded place, out of the public eye, that his greatest work awaited him—translating the Bible into the English language and launching the Lollard movement.

THE BIRTH OF A MOVEMENT

Due to his immense popularity with Oxford students, graduates, and other professors, a significant group of likeminded individuals were drawn to Wycliffe. These were well-educated men who shared his doctrinal convictions concerning the gospel. At this pivotal moment, Wycliffe launched the Lollard movement, which raised up an army of itinerant preachers to proclaim the Word throughout England. So strongly did Wycliffe believe in the necessity of biblical preaching that he personally trained and sent out these men to travel about England to preach the Word. The Lollards were called "evangelical men" by Wycliffe because they proclaimed the *evangel*, the good news of salvation in Jesus Christ.

The term "Lollards" was originally concocted by enemies of the movement as a derisive term meaning "mumbler." It was a pejorative label derived from the Middle Dutch verb *lollen*, "to mumble." To the established Roman Catholic Church, these unlicensed heralds were nothing more than stutterers of nonsense. Despite this scorn, these Bible preachers had a strong effect in spreading the message of salvation in a day when its life-giving truth had been lost.

TRANSLATING THE ENGLISH BIBLE

In the obscurity of Lutterworth, there was an even more important task for Wycliffe to undertake. As Wycliffe invested much of his time into writing tracts that expounded and defended his doctrinal views, he came to realize that the English-speaking people must have the Bible available to them in their own language. In order for the gospel to reach the nation, Wycliffe believed the laity must have the written Word of God in their own native tongue. To this point, the Scriptures had been written exclusively in Latin for only clergy to read and explain to the common people.

In response, Wycliffe initiated the enormous project of translating the entire Bible into Middle English. This monumental undertaking was driven by his deep conviction that the Bible is the Word of God and must be in the hands of the people. The Roman Catholic Church had refused to translate the Bible into the native tongue of Englishmen, lest they lose their spiritual control over them. At this time, all that was available was a Latin Bible, the Vulgate. But the common person could not read Latin. The average English person lived their entire life without ever seeing a copy of the Scripture, much less being able to read it in their own language.

But Wycliffe was determined to change this by launching the momentous task of translating the Bible into English. Once Scripture would be in the hands of the people, he believed that the gospel would spread like wildfire.

WYCLIFFE TAKES THE LEAD

Wycliffe played a significant role in translating the New Testament as the driving force of this project. Wycliffe delegated to other scholars at Oxford the translating work of the Old Testament, and the major part of this work was completed within a year. Under his leadership, this first English Bible was a literal rendering from the Latin Vulgate. The main limitation of this work was that it was translated from the Latin, not from the original Greek and Hebrew.

Once translated, the manuscript had to be meticulously hand-copied, as Johannes Gutenberg had not yet invented the printing press (he would later in 1440). One scribe using a quill, copying a manuscript full-time, required ten months in order to produce one English Bible. The production of hundreds of these Bibles required a large assembly of copyists, who produced a significant number of copies. This was the greatest gift Wycliffe could give to his fellow Englishmen—a Bible in their own language.

LAST DAYS IN ISOLATION

Sadly, England's most influential theologian spent his last

eighteen months in isolation. In the same year, 1382, Wycliffe suffered his first stroke. Though being struck by this setback, he nevertheless persevered in his doctrinal writing, which carefully articulated matters of salvation. This final period of Wycliffe's life proved to be prolific for his writing ministry, which placed him yet again in conflict with the dogma of Rome.

On November 17, 1382, Wycliffe was summoned before a synod at Oxford, which he addressed. In what amounted to a heresy trial, he was excommunicated and commanded to appear in Rome to give an account of his erroneous doctrine. But he refused to acknowledge the authority of the pope and chose to remain in England.

Wycliffe suffered a second stroke on December 28, 1384, leaving him partially immobilized. Any forced journey to Italy was out of the question. His last days on the earth were fast-approaching. While on his deathbed, Wycliffe was visited by his mendicant friar opponents, civil officials, and others, who hoped to hear him recant his beliefs and his confidence that eternal life awaited him. Instead Wycliffe replied, "I shall not die, but live; and shall again declare the evil deeds of the friars."[16] Even in the face of death, his zeal and confidence in Christ burned brightly.

Three days later on New Year's Eve, December 31, 1384,

---

16 Robert Vaughan, *The Tracts and Treatises of John De Wycliffe*, 9.

Wycliffe died. He was buried at the church graveyard in Lutterworth.

WELL-KNOWN IN HEAVEN

At the time Wycliffe departed this world, his name was the object of much scorn in the eyes of the church in Rome. He was condemned as an enemy of the truth, though being the very opposite in the eyes of God. To the English monarchy, Wycliffe was viewed to be a revolutionary who had incited trouble in the nation. In the administration of Oxford, he was regarded as a loose cannon, a threat to the university's reputation. But in the estimation of heaven, Wycliffe was a true champion of the faith, a courageous figure who stood boldly against evil with unwavering resolve and unbending conviction.

The real genius of Wycliffe lay in his firm commitment to the Word of God. He preached, taught, and defended the authority of the Bible in a gloomy day when it was overshadowed by the pope in Rome. Most importantly, he undertook the project of translating the Bible into the language of the English-speaking people. His efforts would pave the way for the Reformation that would eventually follow. For this heroic accomplishment, John Wycliffe will long be recognized as a valiant warrior of the truth of Scripture.

CHAPTER TWO

Bible Defender

In all his arguments, Wycliffe came to stress with growing emphasis that God's Word, the Bible, was the final and only justification for any conclusion.[1]

—G.H.W. PARKER

The influence of John Wycliffe's ministry upon the English-speaking world—and far beyond—lay in his unshakable commitment to the supreme authority of the Bible. His unwavering convictions about the Scripture under-girded all that he taught in the university classroom, wrote in his treatises, and preached in the pulpit. Any understanding of Wycliffe's pivotal role in the history of the church must begin with taking into account his core beliefs concerning the primacy of the Bible. John Wycliffe honored the Word of God

---

[1] G.H.W. Parker, *The Morningstar: Wycliffe and the Dawn of the Reformation* (Grand Rapids, Mich.: Eerdmans, 1965), 42.

above all else, demonstrating a steadfast loyalty to its unerring testimony.

To understand Wycliffe's influence, we must start with his strong belief in what the Reformers would later establish as *sola Scriptura*, a Latin phrase meaning "Scripture alone." This meant that Wycliffe held to the exclusive authority of the written Word of God over all claims of Rome to their authority over church traditions, ecclesiastical councils, and papal renderings. The Bible alone must be regarded as the highest arbiter on all matters. Given the dark times in which Wycliffe lived, the church desperately needed a bold defender of the Word of God—and Wycliffe proved to be that man.

Herbert Workman says, "Wycliffe based everything on the Scriptures"[2] and believed every human voice must yield to this highest authority. Workman adds, "To the objection that the Scriptures were difficult to understand Wycliffe urged that this was only an additional reason for their study."[3] He stresses, "In Wycliffe's judgment, lack of preaching based upon the Word alone, was the cause of spiritual deadness of the age; it was as if one were to prepare a meal without bread. God's Word, especially the gospels, is the seed which brings regeneration and spiritual life."[4] Because of this core belief, Wycliffe

---

2 Herbert B. Workman, *John Wyclif: A Study of the English Medieval Church*, vol. 2 (Oxford, England: Clarendon, 1926), 210.

3 Ibid.

4 Ibid., 211.

devoted his life to establishing the saving truths of the Bible for the English people.

Wycliffe recognized that the people of England were starved for spiritual food. Their feeding on ecclesiastical traditions only made their souls malnourished. Their trust in the papal pontifications had left them emaciated. As in other times in history, fourteenth century England desperately needed the life-giving power of the gospel. From where would this transformation come? The answer would be John Wycliffe.

The Primacy of the Bible

Wycliffe's commitment to the Word was rooted in his unwavering dogmatism that Scripture is infallible revelation from God Himself. Therefore, it alone is authoritative over the church and individual lives. He said, "Holy Scripture is the preeminent authority for every Christian, and the rule of faith and of all human perfection."[5] As a result, the Bible must have the central place in the ministry of the church.

Foundation for All Ministry

This commitment to Scripture shaped Wycliffe's view of ministry. He believed the essence of ministry was not in celebrating the sacraments, but in preaching the written Word of

---

5 "Why Wycliffe Translated the Bible into English," Issue 3, Christian History Institute, accessed May 22, 2020, https://christianhistoryinstitute.org/magazine/article/archives-why-wycliffe-translated.

God.[6] Gotthard Victor Lechler observes Wycliffe's belief in the importance of the Bible, "Before everything else Wycliffe lays stress upon the truth that the preaching of the word of God is that function which serves, in a degree peculiar to itself, to the edification of the Church; and this is so, because the word of God is a seed (Luke viii.11, 'The Seed is the Word of God')."[7] It was this life-giving seed that he purposed to give the primary place in his ministry.

Wycliffe's commitment to Scripture undergirded all his preaching and writing: "O marvelous power of the Divine Seed! Which overpowers strong warriors, softens hard hearts, and renews, and makes divine, men brutalized by sin, and departed infinitely far from God. Plainly, so mighty a wonder could never be wrought by the word of a priest, if the Spirit of Life and the Eternal Word did not, above all things else, work with it."[8]

Wycliffe believed in the divine power of the gospel message to convert and transform the lives of his fellow man. Contrary to the tradition-based messages of his day, he insisted that such supernatural "wonder" can only come from the Holy Spirit working through the Scriptures. To the written Word of God, Wycliffe dedicated himself with indefatigable resolve. He knew that England could never be converted to

---

6   Nicholas R. Needham, *2000 Years of Christ's Power*, vol. 2 (Fearn, Ross-shire, Scotland: Christian Focus, 2017), 418.

7   Gotthard Victor Lechler and Peter Lorimer, *John Wycliffe and His English Precursors* (London: The Religious Tract Society, 1884), 178.

8   Ibid.

Jesus Christ apart from the preaching of the Word. Lechler continues, "It was this prevailing want of the true seed of the Word of life which, in his opinion, was to blame for the spiritual deadness of the people, and for the wickedness which in consequence prevailed in the world."[9] Without the truth of Christ to impart life, Wycliffe's country would continue to be a spiritual graveyard, filled with religious corpses.

In Defense of the Truth

As Wycliffe assessed the state of England, the problem was not simply an absence of the Word of God. The danger was much more dire. The church in his native land was actually standing in direct opposition to the truth of the Word. In his work titled "Wycliffe's Wicket," Wycliffe frames the issue: "And they say it is heresy to express the holy Scripture in English, but in saying so they would condemn the Holy Ghost who gave tongues to Christ's apostles so they could speak the Word of God in all languages that were ordained of God under heaven."[10] This inaccessibility of Scripture was in direct conflict with God.

For Wycliffe, denying the primacy and accessibility of the Word was a frontal assault upon God Himself, whose authority undergirds the Bible. He maintains:

> Consider whether it is not the same thing to deny Christ's words as heresy, as it is to make Christ a

---

9   Ibid., 180.

10   John Wycliffe, *Wycliffe's Wickett*.

heretic; for if my word is a lie then I am a liar if I speak that word. Therefore if my words are heresy, then I am a heretic if I speak the words; therefore it is the same thing to condemn the word of God in any language as heresy, and God as an heretic, who spoke the word.[11]

This absence of Scripture was—and remains today—a slippery slope that descends into eternal punishment.

THE ATTRIBUTES OF THE BIBLE

What was Wycliffe's core understanding of the Bible itself? He rightly recognized Scripture as the foundational basis for everything he believed and taught. It was this pre-Reformer's strong conviction about the Scriptures that enabled them to hold such vital importance in his thinking. Wycliffe strongly believed in the Bible's inspiration, inerrancy, unity, authority, and ability to judge.

Divine Inspiration

In a day when the pope claimed to speak on behalf of God, Wycliffe affirmed the divine inspiration of the Bible alone. He believed that God's Word is a living book, containing the breath of God Himself. He wrote, "God's word is the life of the world, and every word of God is the life of the human

---

11   Ibid.

soul."[12] Thus, Wycliffe was convinced that whenever someone receives the truth of God by faith, he receives divine life into his spiritually dead soul. The Bible alone, Wycliffe claimed, is the only living book that implants eternal life to the barren soul. No religious leader or church tradition has that life-giving and soul-saving power—not even the pope.

Perfect Inerrancy

Wycliffe was also convinced that the Bible speaks with the absolute truthfulness of God, who cannot lie. The divinely inspired Word can never speak what is false. His Word cannot contain any error or distortion of reality, because the Bible is from the mouth of God. Wycliffe held it must be perfectly inerrant in all it teaches. He wrote: "The Holy Scripture is the faultless, most true, most perfect, and most holy law of God, which it is the duty of all men to learn, to know, to defend, and to observe."[13] Simply put, Wycliffe believed the Bible speaks with unadulterated truth.

Writing on the inerrancy of Scripture in his book *On the Truth of Holy Scripture*, Wycliffe wrote, "For if God, who cannot lie, has spoken something in his own Scripture, which is itself the mirror of his will, then it is true."[14] Wycliffe repeat-

---

12 *The Life and Times of John Wycliffe* (London: Religious Tract Society, 1884), 130.

13 George R. Crooks and John Fletcher Hurst, *History of the Christian Church*, vol. 2 (New York: Eaton & Mains, 1900), 36.

14 John Wycliffe, *On the Truth of Holy Scripture*, trans. Ian Christopher Levy, in *John Wycliffe on the Truth of Holy Scripture* (Kalamazoo, Mich.: Medieval Institute Publications, 2001), 200.

edly affirmed the Scripture to be without any mixture of error: "It is impossible for any part of the Holy Scripture to be wrong. In Holy Scripture is all the truth."[15] This commitment that the Bible speaks without any error deepened his resolve that the gospel will go forth in life-changing power.

Absolute Sufficiency

For Wycliffe, understanding that God had perfectly revealed Himself in Scripture also meant that what had been revealed was sufficient for the salvation and sanctification of everyone who believes it. He said, "Everything necessary is found in Scripture, and what is not there is unnecessary."[16]

Though many in the church promoted philosophies and ideas rooted in tradition, Wycliffe consistently maintained that which is of ultimate benefit came from Scripture alone. He wrote in *On the Truth of Holy Scripture*, "It is evident from the faith of Scripture, which one must believe, that a person can acquire nothing superior, nor more certain or efficacious. Indeed, since the entirety of Holy Scripture is the word of the Lord, no testimony could possibly be better, more certain, or more efficacious."[17]

---

15 David Fountain, *John Wycliffe: The Dawn of the Reformation* (United Kingdom: Mayflower Christian, 1984), 48.

16 John Wycliffe, Sermon 92/58, 93/77, 120/16, quoted in *English Wycliffite Sermons*, vol. 4, eds. Pamela Gordon and Anne Hudson (Oxford, England: Clarendon, 1996), 71.

17 John Wycliffe, *On the Truth of Holy Scripture*, trans. Ian Christopher Levy, in *John Wycliffe on the Truth of Holy Scripture* (Kalamazoo, Mich.: Medieval Institute Publications, 2001), 200.

Internal Unity

Wycliffe further stressed the perfect internal unity of Scripture. He affirmed: "The whole Scripture is one word of God; also the whole law of Christ is one perfect word proceeding from the mouth of God."[18] Scripture is never self-contradictory, but speaks with one voice. Wycliffe was convinced the Scripture is one colorful tapestry, with every thread woven into its perfect place. From beginning to end, the Word of God gives one consistent testimony to the truth, never contradicting itself.

Because of this intrinsic consistency, Wycliffe stressed that the Scripture best interprets itself.[19] That is to say, it perfectly explains itself. He claimed that the Bible is its own best interpreter because Scripture best elucidates its own truths to the reader.

Supreme Authority

In a critical hour when the church was considered to be its own highest authority, Wycliffe attested to the supreme right of the Bible to rule all lives. He elevated the Scripture above church leaders and over even the pope himself. He stated: "It alone is the supreme law that is to rule church, state, and Christian life, without traditions and statutes."[20] Here, he

---

18 John Laird Wilson, *John Wycliffe: Patriot and Reformer* (New York: Funk & Wagnalls, 1884), 232.

19 Fountain, 48.

20 "Why Wycliffe Translated the Bible Into English," *Christianity Today*, accessed July 20, 2020, https://www.christianitytoday.com/history/issues/issue-3/from-archives -why-wycliffe-translated-bible-into-english.html.

states his fundamental belief that every human tradition must yield to the higher authority of Scripture. Likewise, every man and religious custom in the church must submit itself to the overruling sovereignty of the Bible.

Wycliffe contended that Scripture holds preeminent authority in all that it teaches. He stated, "It is a doctrine of the faith that Christ is infinitely superior to every other man, and therefore His book, or Holy Scripture, which is His law, stands in a similar relation to every other writing which can be named."[21] As Christ is Lord over the church, His written Word rules over every lesser opinion or long-standing tradition of man. In *On the Truth of Holy Scripture*, Wycliffe writes, "Therefore, just as all rivers flow to the sea, so all created authority depends upon the authority of the First Master."[22]

Final Judge

Wycliffe also believed the Scripture is the final judge in all spiritual matters in the life of the church. In *The Truth of Holy Scripture*, written in 1378, Wycliffe proclaimed the Bible as the ultimate norm by which the church, tradition, councils, and even the pope must be tested. It is the measuring rod by which all matters of faith and practice are compared. Whatever the decisions of the church, they must comply with the governance of the Word. Wycliffe wrote: "As they ought to be, the papal

---

21 Lechler and Lorimer, *John Wycliffe and His English Precursors*, 236.

22 John Wycliffe, *On the Truth of Holy Scripture*, trans. Ian Christopher Levy, in *John Wycliffe on the Truth of Holy Scripture* (Kalamazoo, Mich.: Medieval Institute Publications, 2001), 200.

bulls will be superseded by the Holy Scriptures. The veneration of men for the laws of the papacy, as well as for the opinions of our modern doctors . . . will be restrained within due limits. What concern have the faithful with writings of this sort, except that they are honestly deduced from the fountain of Scripture?"[23]

To one papal bull issued by Pope Gregory, Wycliffe responded: "These conclusions have I delivered as a grain of faith separated from the chaff by which the ungrateful tares are set on fire. These, opposed to the Scriptures of truth, like the crimson blossom of a foul revenge, provide sustenance for Antichrist. Of this the infallible sign is, that there reigns in the clergy a Luciferian enmity and pride, consisting in the lust of domination, the wife of which is covetousness of earthly things, breeding together the children of the fiend, the children of evangelical poverty being no more."[24]

Wycliffe shone the light of God's Word into the man-centered abyss of false teaching. Having confronted the power structure of the apostate church of his day, Wycliffe's work demonstrates the preeminent power of the Word of God to carry out the fruitful work of God.

THE POWER OF THE BIBLE

Because the Bible is the living Word of Sovereign God, as it claims to be, it comes with the same power that belongs

---

23 Wilson, 233.
24 Vaughan, *The Tracts and Treatises of John De Wycliffe*, Li.

exclusively to Him. In other words, the supreme power of God Himself is the very might contained in His Word.

Reproving Power

Wycliffe believed the Bible possesses reproving power to correct all error unaligned with its teaching. He wrote: "By pursuing such a course it is not only in our power to reduce the mandates of prelates and popes to their just place, but the errors of these new religious orders also might be corrected and the worship of Christ well purified and elevated."[25]

Wycliffe insisted that every aspect of the church and individual believers are subject to the scrutiny and rebuke of the Bible. Every falsehood in the church must be corrected by holy Scripture, whether it be doctrinal or ethical error. Even if the fallacy is promoted by the highest church authorities, it must be confronted and corrected by the "Thus says the Lord" of the Bible.

Saving Power

Wycliffe believed the Word of God possesses the power to regenerate sinners who are spiritually dead in trespasses and sin. Because like produces like, only the living Word of Christ can impart new life to spiritual corpses. The written Word is used by the Holy Spirit to produce regeneration in those who are without spiritual breath.

---

25 Wilson, 233.

For Wycliffe, the written Word could not be separated from the saving person and work of Jesus Christ, the living Word. He said, "Forasmuch as the Bible contains Christ, that is all that is necessary for salvation, it is necessary for all men, not for priests alone."[26] Thus, Wycliffe dedicated his life to spreading the soul-saving Word of God to all men, whether to priests or paupers. He believed that his calling from God was to provide an English Bible that was accessible to the common person of his day. In this way, he provided an invaluable gift for his generation to learn the gospel through the study of His Word.

The Knowledge of Christ

Concerning this commitment, Parker writes, "In itself it was perfectly sufficient for salvation, without the addition of customs or traditions such as canon law, prayers to the saints, fastings, pilgrimages or the Mass. . . . Knowledge of the Bible alone was essential, he argued, and failure to know it was failure to know Christ."[27] In salvation, Wycliffe believed the knowledge of Christ cannot be separated from the Bible. The written Word and the living Word are inseparably joined together in ministry.

In Wycliffe's thinking, the test of true conversion evidenced itself "when a man will gladly and willingly hear the word of God; when he knoweth himself prepared to do good

---

26 Stephen J. Lang, Kenneth A. Curtis, and Randy Petersen, *The 100 Most Important Events in Christian History* (Grand Rapids, Mich.: Revell, 2005), 87.

27 John Wycliffe, *De Veritate Sacrae Scripturae*, quoted in Parker, *The Morning Star: Wycliffe and the Dawn of the Reformation*, 43.

works; when he is willing to flee sin; when a man can be sorry for his sin."[28] Wycliffe believed the Bible identifies important parameters for those who receive salvation. Having Scripture in the language of the common people would enable them to examine their spiritual state more effectively. This translation of the Bible would help equip individuals in their faith for centuries to come.

THE INTERPRETATION OF THE BIBLE

The Bible must be studied and interpreted with diligent care, Wycliffe believed. He understood that it must be read and understood in a literal, straightforward manner unless reason dictated otherwise. Wycliffe stated, "Now in this matter I have often stated that Scripture is true in all its parts according to the intended literal sense. This is why professors of Holy Scripture ought to imitate its manner of speaking, adhering to its eloquence and logic, more so than any foreign pagan writing."[29]

Plain Meaning

After centuries of the medieval church allegorizing the Bible, Wycliffe insisted that the plain meaning of Scripture must be sought and believed. He stated, "It is, therefore, not permitted

---

28 Vaughan, *The Tracts and Treatises of John De Wycliffe*, 2.

29 John Wycliffe, *On the Truth of Holy Scripture*, trans. Ian Christopher Levy, in *John Wycliffe on the Truth of Holy Scripture* (Kalamazoo, Mich.: Medieval Institute Publications, 2001), 41.

to sever the Holy Scripture, but to allege it in its integrity according to the sense of the author."[30] Here, he expounds that the correct interpretation of Scripture is rooted and grounded in its authorial intent. He stressed that the message of Scripture must be taken at face value. It must not be twisted to find an obscure meaning that God never intended.

On the recovery of a literal hermeneutic by Wycliffe, Kantik Ghosh makes this observation: "Wycliffe gives theoretical centrality to a concept of the Bible as a unique text, demanding from the reader a constant and significant awareness of its separate hermeneutic status. Such a reader is expected to attempt to understand the Bible 'literally,' which in Lollard theory involves accessing the divine intention."[31] This divine intention is what drove Wycliffe's theology of the inspired Word. It is wholly inerrant and the reader must be submitted to its literal and authoritative truths.

Concerning Wycliffe, Ghosh goes on to say, "'Inspiration' [from the Holy Spirit] and 'open reason' form the twin exegetical positives; they are the necessary correctives to the human propensity to become false glossators of God's Word."[32] So strong was Wycliffe's reverence for the inspiration and authority of Scripture that he lived with "a governing fear" over the

---

30 John Fletcher Hurst, *History of the Christian Church* (New York: Eaton & Mains, 1900), 36.
31 Kantik Ghosh, *The Wycliffite Heresy: Authority and Interpretation of Texts* (Cambridge, England: Cambridge University Press, 2004), 149.
32 Ibid.

"possibility of 'imposing' an alien [human] hermeneutic or a fallen logic on the Bible."[33]

Single Meaning

Because Wycliffe was committed to a plain interpretation, it follows that he believed every passage has only one interpretation—the literal sense. There was no place in the study of the Bible for the tortuous interpretations that were common to his day. The medieval church had sunk into the mire of allegorizing the Bible. Its priests were famous for spiritualizing the biblical text in order to find a hidden meaning. The straightforward meaning was being discarded in favor of an imposed meaning.

Against this human sophistry Wycliffe said, "It is evident from the faith of Scripture, which one must believe, that a person can acquire nothing superior, nor more certain or efficacious. . . . For if God, who cannot lie, has spoken something in his own Scripture, which is itself the mirror of his will, then it is true."[34] According to Wycliffe, the plain meaning of Scripture was available to all men by faith and dependence upon the Holy Spirit to illumine their understanding to God's intent and meaning.[35] It was the priests who confused the simple meaning of Scripture. He continued his instruction by

---

33 Ibid.

34 John Wycliffe, *On the Truth of Holy Scripture*, trans. Ian Christopher Levy, in *John Wycliffe on the Truth of Holy Scripture* (Kalamazoo, Mich.: Medieval Institute Publications, 2001), 200.

35 Ibid.

saying, "It is absolutely essential that every person be a theologian, having first set his own affections in proper order. For then the Truth will deign to descend and instruct him in manner free from all deception."[36]

But Wycliffe resisted this contrived practice, which involved more imagination than interpretation. He chose to pursue the one meaning that was intended by the biblical author. This marked a dramatic shift toward the interpretation that sought the single meaning of a biblical passage.

Linguistic Meaning

Wycliffe ardently supported a direct approach to explaining the Bible. He wrote against the introduction of new words into the Christian's understanding of Scripture. Wycliffe chose to restrict himself to the use of biblical words as much as he could. It could easily obfuscate the meaning of Scripture to use non-biblical words that are void of precise biblical meaning. Wycliffe stated: "It should be observed that when it came to drawing upon linguistic novelties, the holy doctors of the Early Church quite reasonably forbade, in matters of faith, the introduction of new-fangled terms which are foreign to Scripture, for fear of the poison which could be hidden in them by heretics. . . . The safest route, therefore, is to employ the terms and logic of Scripture."[37]

---

36 Ibid.

37 John Wycliffe, *On the Truth of Holy Scripture*, trans. Ian Christopher Levy, in *John Wycliffe on the Truth of Holy Scripture* (Kalamazoo, Mich.: Medieval Institute Publications, 2001), 181.

It was also common in Wycliffe's day for scholars and pastors to become entangled in the web of philosophic extractions about truth, without actually speaking the words of truth. Wycliffe, being a plain-spoken man of the truth, resisted such rhetorical traditions by saying, "The Christian should speak the words of Scripture under the authority of Scripture, and according to that form which Scripture itself illustrates."[38] His conviction that the Word of God should stand alone in its clear meaning would motivate and shape everything about his life and ministry.

THE PRACTICE OF THE BIBLE

Wycliffe believed that every ministry of the church and aspect of daily life should be directed by the teaching of Scripture. Having translated the Bible into the common language of the people, Wycliffe instructed his followers in the proper use of Scripture. He wrote, "Obtain a reliable text, understand the logic of Scripture, compare the parts of Scripture with one another, maintain an attitude of humble seeking, and receive the instruction of the Spirit."[39]

---

38   John Wycliffe, *On the Truth of Holy Scripture*, trans. Ian Christopher Levy, in *John Wycliffe on the Truth of Holy Scripture* (Kalamazoo, Mich.: Medieval Institute Publications, 2001), 69.

39   "Why Wycliffe Translated the Bible into English," Issue 3, Christian History Institute, accessed July 16, 2020, https://christianhistoryinstitute.org/magazine/article/archives-why-wycliffe-translated.

Allegiance to the Scripture

Though the spirit of the age was drifting away from the preaching and application of the Bible as it was to be plainly understood, Wycliffe advocated for it all the more. He said, "Now if anyone sins he fails to believe in God, and thus lacks the first article of faith. . . . Forsaking the faith of Scripture is the first cause of wickedness."[40] Wycliffe affirmed that an allegiance to the teaching of Scripture is non-negotiable: "I say here that it is necessary to preach all the way to the very ends of the earth. The more strength sin gathers, the more essential it is to preaching, since it is certainly impossible for anyone to sin unless he lacks faith."[41]

Necessary for Holy Living

This high view of Scripture led Wycliffe to insist on its sufficiency to direct the believer into holy living. He wrote, "For it is essential that every Christian learn the faith of the Church. . . . Otherwise, he would not be a person of faith, and faith is the highest theology of all."[42] Wycliffe contended that per-

---

40 John Wycliffe, *On the Truth of Holy Scripture*, trans. Ian Christopher Levy, in *John Wycliffe on the Truth of Holy Scripture* (Kalamazoo, Mich.: Medieval Institute Publications, 2001), 291–92.

41 John Wycliffe, *On the Truth of Holy Scripture*, trans. Ian Christopher Levy, in *John Wycliffe on the Truth of Holy Scripture* (Kalamazoo, Mich.: Medieval Institute Publications, 2001), 291.

42 John Wycliffe, *On the Truth of Holy Scripture*, trans. Ian Christopher Levy, in *John Wycliffe on the Truth of Holy Scripture* (Kalamazoo, Mich.: Medieval Institute Publications, 2001), 300.

sonal godliness would be realized only when it is carried out in obedience to the Bible.

The reality of Christlikeness is produced in the believer by the transforming power of the Word of God. The Scripture contains the life-giving power of God that must be rightly applied and personally lived. The Scripture must be applied to everyday life and lived out in the power of the Holy Spirit. In short, Wycliffe believed that every Christian must be a living epistle whose life resembles the truth of the Bible.

The Defense of the Bible

As a preacher of the Word, Wycliffe upheld its truths so that God's people would be spiritually matured and set free. He wrote, "Oh, if God would only grant me a docile heart, one marked by perseverance, steadfastness, and love for Christ and his church, and even for those members of the devil who so mangle the church of Christ, that I might rebuke them with a pure love! How glorious a cause it would be for me to put an end to this present misery!"[43]

His defense of the Bible upheld his personal piety and those to whom he ministered. He wrote, "It is absolutely essential that every person be a theologian, having first set his own affections in proper order. For then the Truth will deign to descend and instruct him in manner free from all

---

43 John Wycliffe, *On the Truth of Holy Scripture*, trans. Ian Christopher Levy, in *John Wycliffe on the Truth of Holy Scripture* (Kalamazoo, Mich.: Medieval Institute Publications, 2001), 298.

deception. . . . Indeed, since God speaks every truth, clearly his speech is the First Cause of any and all extrinsic truth. . . . And so it seems to me that all other evidence which does not lead back to this principle is deceptive."[44]

BACK TO THE BIBLE

Wycliffe was the trailblazing forerunner who pioneered the way for English readers to study the Bible for themselves and apply it to their lives. This marked the beginning of the light of truth to shine into the darkened lives of his countrymen. The psalmist writes, "Your word is a lamp to my feet and a light to my path" (Ps. 119:105). Solomon affirms the same, "For the commandment is a lamp and the teaching is light" (Prov. 6:23). This light was now, at last, beginning to blaze across England—and Wycliffe was its torchbearer. Through the many translations of the Scripture into the English language that would follow—from the Tyndale Bible to the King James Bible, to the modern English version—Wycliffe would soon be regarded as the one who brought the precious truths of the Bible to the English-speaking world.

---

44 John Wycliffe, *On the Truth of Holy Scripture*, trans. Ian Christopher Levy, in *John Wycliffe on the Truth of Holy Scripture* (Kalamazoo, Mich.: Medieval Institute Publications, 2001), 200–201.

CHAPTER THREE

Bible
Theologian

John Wycliffe was the most eminent Oxford theologian of his day . . . a keen Bible student, a scholarly commentator on the sacred text.[1]

—F.F BRUCE

A survey of the writings of John Wycliffe reveals he was staunchly Reformed in his theology. Because of Wycliffe's careful study of Scripture, he was deeply persuaded of these convictions long before the Reformation began. The core doctrines that this Oxford professor taught would become more fully developed by the magisterial Reformers. But Wycliffe, nevertheless, played a strategic role in laying the sturdy foundation upon which the Protestant movement would later be built.

Noted theologian Loraine Boettner comments on the doctrinal teaching of Wycliffe: "Wycliffe was a Reformer of the

---

1   F.F. Bruce, *The History of the English Bible* (Cambridge, England: Lutterworth, 2002), 12.

Calvinistic type, proclaiming the absolute sovereignty of God and the foreordination of all things. His system of belief was very similar to that which was later taught by Luther and Calvin."[2] Prior to Calvin stepping onto the world stage, Wycliffe had already embraced the same essential tenets of Reformed truth drawn from Scripture. If Martin Luther and John Calvin were the fathers of the Reformation, John Wycliffe was the spiritual grandfather of the Reformation.

This famed Bible translator affirmed the fundamental doctrines that later became known as the doctrines of grace. Based upon the authority of Scripture, Wycliffe affirmed that salvation is by grace alone, through faith alone, in Christ alone. This orthodoxy earned him the grand title of "The Evangelical Doctor." Wycliffe proclaimed the true gospel and upheld it in the midst of the many heretical errors of his day. His theological convictions were securely anchored to Scripture at a time when the church had drifted from its doctrinal moorings and was sinking in an open sea of apostasy.

THE DOCTRINE OF GOD

In theology proper, Wycliffe upheld the vital cornerstone truth that God is the supreme Lord of heaven and earth. He affirmed that God, by His sovereign will, brought all things into being by the breath of His power. Having created the entire universe and

---

2   Loraine Boettner, *The Reformed Doctrine of Predestination* (Phillipsburg, N.J.: Presbyterian and Reformed, 1991), 367.

all it contains, God presides over the works of His hands and directs all things, great or small, according to His providence.

Wycliffe possessed a profound sense of God's transcendent majesty, and he taught that this must be a man's greatest focus in cultivating spiritual maturity. He wrote in his tract "A Short Rule of Life," "First, when thou risest, or fully wakest, think upon the goodness of thy God; how for His own goodness, and not for any need, He made all things out of nothing, both angels and men, and all other creatures, good in their kind."[3]

Omnipotent Creator

While many in the fourteenth century held fanciful ideas about the origin of the world, Wycliffe held fast to the biblical account: "In the beginning God created the heavens and the earth" (Gen. 1:1). In observing this foundational truth, he wrote, "We should believe that God the Father, being almighty, without beginning and ending, made heaven and earth, and all creatures, of naught, through His word."[4] Wycliffe's strong conviction affirmed that he believed in God's omnipotence, eternality, and sovereignty. Being all-powerful, God effortlessly made everything out of nothing. This fundamental belief once again confirmed Wycliffe's unwavering commitment to a literal understanding of Scripture.

---

3 John Wycliffe, *Writings of the Reverend and Learned John Wickliff* (London: Religious Tract Society, 1831), 149.

4 John Wycliffe, *Writings of the Reverend and Learned John Wickliff* (London: Religious Tract Society, 1831), 53.

Eternal Decreer

Rather than seeing the world in uncontrolled chaos, Wycliffe believed that whatever God foreordained in eternity past must come to pass. He taught, "By arguments of this kind also, we [show] other events to be necessary, the coming of which has been determined by God."[5] Wycliffe understood that the decretive will of God is known exclusively to Him. He explained: "Nor will it matter, after what manner God may choose to inform us, that He had actually so determined before the foundation of the world."[6] He explained that God has revealed to man only part of what He has ordained will occur. Whatever He has determined to do before the world began, Wycliffe maintained, it will surely come to pass according to His eternal decree.

Sovereign Ruler

Wycliffe likewise emphasized that God continually rules over all that He has made. In one sermon, he asserted, "Everything must happen as God has ordained."[7] The converse is also true. He stated, "Nothing can happen in this world unless God has ordained it."[8] He believed that nothing can hinder

---

5   Robert Vaughan, *The Life and Opinions of John de Wycliffe*, vol. 2 (London: B.J. Holdsworth, 1828), 354.

6   Ibid.

7   John Wycliffe, Sermon 179/56, 194/6, quoted in *English Wycliffite Sermons,* vol. 4, eds. Pamela Gordon and Anne Hudson (Oxford, England: Clarendon, 1996), 57.

8   John Wycliffe, Sermon 107/20, 108/49, quoted in *English Wycliffite Sermons,* vol. 4, eds. Pamela Gordon and Anne Hudson (Oxford, England: Clarendon, 1996), 57.

the predetermined plan of God, which extends over all people and events in every place. He wrote: "Let it be certain, that God has predetermined an event, and the result is beyond all accident, it must follow. Now what could hinder this preordination of events on the part of God? His knowledge is perfect. His will unvarying. And all creature-impediments opposed to Him are futile. From these facts, it follows that whatsoever is future, must necessarily come."[9]

Wycliffe made crystal clear his firm belief in the doctrine of divine predestination—that God brings to pass whatever occurs, whether He directly causes it or He permissively allows it. Either way, God remains sovereign over its occurrence. This was a truth Wycliffe did not hesitate to declare. A supposed "accident," he writes, is actually a part of a larger, much more complex plan of God. To this end, Wycliffe believed that nothing can thwart nor alter the eternal purpose of God.

THE DOCTRINE OF CHRIST

Regarding the second person of the Trinity, Wycliffe affirmed that Jesus Christ was sent by the Father into this fallen world in order to rescue those perishing in their sins. In his Christology, Wycliffe was entirely orthodox according to the ancient creeds that articulated Jesus was truly God and truly man, the God-man, both Lord and Savior.

---

9   Ibid.

Second Adam

Wycliffe understood Jesus Christ to be the second Adam, who succeeded through His perfect obedience where the first Adam failed by disobedience. Therefore, Jesus had to become a man in order to succeed in the same manner that Adam failed. Without the incarnation of Christ, Wycliffe reasoned, "The satisfaction for the sin of the first man would not have been adequate."[10] Therefore, Jesus, who made propitiation for our sins, had to enter into the same human race as Adam. Where the first man transgressed the law of God, the second Adam must obey in order to redeem fallen humanity from the curse of the law.

Infallible Prophet

Wycliffe taught that in His incarnation, Jesus spoke infallible truth that had been given to Him by the Father. He said: "If Christ prophesied of certain events, certainly to come, such events have been or will be. The antecedent, namely that Christ has thus prophesied, is necessary, and the consequence is also necessary."[11]

By this statement, Wycliffe asserted that there is divine necessity in the fulfillment of all Christ has prophesied. All that was taught by Jesus Christ must come to pass. Whatever He spoke can never fail or falter. He wrote: "The consequence is

---

10 Jaroslav Pelikan, *The Christian Tradition: A History of the Development of Doctrine*, vol. 4, *Reformation of Church and Dogma, 1300–1700* (Chicago: University of Chicago Press, 2012), 24.

11 Ibid.

not in the power of any man, or of any creature; nor are the sayings of Christ, or the elections of His mind to be affected by accident. And therefore as it is necessary that Christ has foretold certain things, so it is necessary they should come to pass."[12]

Wycliffe believed that when Christ speaks what the Father has given to Him to say, it must perfectly come to pass. Jesus speaks as an infallible prophet who never erred in what He spoke.

Sinless Substitute

Wycliffe further taught that Jesus Christ was the perfectly sinless Son of God without spot or blemish. His absolute holiness qualified Him to die in the place of guilty, hell-bound sinners. He wrote, "All this He did and suffered of His own kindness, without any sin of Himself, that He might deliver us from sin and pain, and bring us to everlasting bliss."[13] In other words, Jesus Christ had to be sinless in order to be a perfect Substitute and appease the wrath of holy God toward sinners.

Wycliffe affirmed, "Christ died not for His own sins as thieves do for theirs, but as our brother, who Himself might not sin, He died for the sins that others had done."[14] He stressed the vicarious nature of His death for those who could not save themselves. For his day, this theology was revolutionary, in that it recovered the roots of orthodox Christianity

---

12 Ibid.

13 *Life and Times of John de Wycliffe*, 67.

14 Ibid.

that had been lost in the corruption of the church tradition of Rome.

The believer's devotion to Christ is deepened by the truth of the substitutionary death of Christ. Wycliffe offered practical encouragement to followers of Christ: "Think on the great sufferings and willing death the Christ suffered for mankind. When no man might make satisfaction for the guilt of Adam and Eve, and others more, neither any angel might make satisfaction therefore, the Christ, of his endless charity, suffered such great passion and painful death, that no creature could suffer so much."[15]

In these words, Wycliffe points to the overflowing love of Christ to endure such a horrific death, in order to propitiate the wrath of God toward His people.

Suffering Savior

Wycliffe taught that the crucifixion of Jesus Christ was a dreadful death in which He suffered greatly. Wycliffe strongly affirmed that the saving purpose in this traumatic event was to bring about the redemption of all who would believe in the Lord Jesus. Wycliffe wrote: "He was lifted up on the cross and died for sinners, to deliver us from the tormenting of the devil. He suffered pain to deliver us from everlasting pain. He suffered death to deliver us from death."[16]

---

15 John Wycliffe, *Writings of the Reverend and Learned John Wickliff* (London: The Religious Tract Society, 1831), 149.

16 Wycliffe, *Writings of the Reverend and Learned John Wickliff,* 104.

In this statement, Wycliffe asserted that Jesus paid a great price—He "suffered pain" upon the cross—in order to ransom sinners. Christ did so in order to deliver believers from the eternal wrath of God.

Wycliffe went on to poignantly describe the suffering of Christ for the Christian in his tract "Expositio Decalogi":

And remember heartily of the wonderful kindness of God, who was so high and worshipful in heaven, that He should come down so low, and be born of the maiden, and become our brother to buy us again by His hard passion, from our servitude of the devil. He was beaten, buffeted, and scourged. He was crowned with a crown of thorns for despite, and when the crown, as clerks say, could not sit fast, and close down to his head, for the long and stiff thorns, they took staves and beat them down, till the thorns pierced the place of the brain. He was nailed hand and foot, and with nails sharp and rugged, that His pain should be the more, and so at last he suffered a painful death, hanging full shamefully on the hard tree. . . . It should be full sweet and delightful to us to think thus on this great kindness and this great love of Jesus Christ.[17]

---

17 John Wycliffe, *Expositio Decalogi*.

Marveling at such amazing grace, Wycliffe reminds the believer the great cost of their salvation—and how it is great reason to worship Him.

Exclusive Mediator

In his teaching, Wycliffe was unwavering in his conviction that Jesus is the only Mediator between sinful mankind and holy God. He stated: "For as the Scripture assures us, Christ is the only mediator between God and man."[18] A mediator is one who negotiates peace between two parties at enmity with each other. In this regard, Wycliffe believed in the exclusivity of salvation in Christ. There is no other means of finding acceptance with God except through the sole mediation of the Son of God.

Resurrected Lord

Wycliffe also taught that Jesus Christ was raised from the dead. This guarantees the final resurrection of all people to stand before Him on the last day. Wycliffe wrote, "He again rose from death, that we should again rise in body and soul on the last day of the great doom."[19] Jesus was raised in order to be seated at the Father's right hand and rule over all creation. Christ will preside as Judge over the world on "the last day of the great doom." Wycliffe held to these truths tenaciously, forging the path ahead for faithful Christians to come.

---

18   L. Laurenson, *Wycliffe's Work for England* (N.P.: Irving Risch, 2015), n.p.
19   Wycliffe, *Writings of the Reverend and Learned John Wickliff*, 104.

The Doctrine of Sin

Further, Wycliffe taught the radical corruption of sin in the fallen human nature of every person. Following the teaching of Scripture, he held to the cardinal doctrines of original sin, total depravity, and eternal punishment.

Original Sin

When the first man Adam sinned, Wycliffe taught that he was without excuse. This defiant act of original sin brought God's severe punishment upon him and the entire human race. Wycliffe maintained: "God bade Adam not to eat of the apple; but he broke God's command; and he was not excused therein, neither by his own folly, (or weakness), or by Eve, nor by the serpent. And thus by the righteousness of God, this sin must always be punished."[20]

By this one sin of disobedience to God, Adam fell into an immediate state of condemnation. Wycliffe wrote, "Adam indulged pride so as to bring death upon himself voluntarily."[21] The first man sinned arrogantly, causing him to presume he was above the law of God. But his solitary sin brought death to himself.

Wycliffe also taught that Adam's original sin was imputed to all men. As our representative, the penalty that was assigned to him fell on all his descendants. Wycliffe succinctly states,

---

20 Wycliffe, *Writings of the Reverend and Learned John Wickliff*, 186.
21 Ibid., 181.

"by Adam all die."[22] When the first man sinned, death spread to the entire human race. The act of this one man brought death to all. This doctrine is known as federal headship, which Wycliffe held to unabashedly.

Divine Punishment

Wycliffe taught that the sin of Adam brought a devastating effect upon his own standing before God. He believed that Adam's defiant rebellion incurred divine punishment. He wrote: "By the righteousness of God, this sin must always be punished."[23] The just penalty for Adam's sin of cosmic treason was the full curse of the law, which was death in its every form—spiritual, physical, and eternal death. Tragically, death spread to all people through this one act of sin.

Universal Depravity

Wycliffe held that Adam's sin caused depravity to permeate the entirety of every person's human nature. He believed that Adam's sin nature is passed down from parent to child at the moment of each person's conception in the womb. Wycliffe wrote: "We are all originally sinners, as Adam, and in Adam; his leprosy cleaves to us faster than Naaman's did to Gehazi."[24] Here Wycliffe believed that Adam's one act of disobedience plunged the entire human race into spiritual ruin. He stated: "Man was

---

22 Vaughan, *Tracts and Treatises of John de Wycliffe*, 159.
23 Wycliffe, *Writings of the Reverend and Learned John Wickliff*, 186.
24 Wycliffe, *Writings of the Reverend and Learned John Wickliff*, 42.

ruined by the forbidden fruit of a tree."[25] Because of Adam's sin, all people have been totally defiled in their inner nature.

Corrupted Mind

In Wycliffe's thinking, as a result of inheriting a sin nature, every person's mind has been blinded toward spiritual matters. He taught, "We are all sinners, not only from our birth, but before, so that we cannot so much as think a good thought."[26] Because the tainted pollution of sin resides in every person, no person can think rightly about God or themselves. The repercussions of this transmitted corruption have disabled human mental faculty from functioning as it was created—to love and honor God first.

Enslaved Will

Wycliffe similarly maintained that the will of every unbeliever is enslaved by the devil. He wrote, "Wicked men are called the kingdom of the devil, for he reigns in them, and they do his will."[27] He reasoned from Scripture that no one possesses moral ability or free will to choose to do good toward God, because Satan holds every unconverted person captive under the tyranny of his evil dominion. Therefore, Wycliffe stressed that all men are imprisoned in sin and are entirely self-absorbed. He writes, "Man is the most fallen of creatures,

---

25 Ibid., 181.
26 Ibid., 42.
27 Ibid., 89.

and the unkindest of all creatures that ever God made!"[28] He concluded that sin has utterly consumed man with self-love, being self-absorbed, devoid of any sacrificial love toward God or others.

THE DOCTRINE OF SALVATION

Wycliffe believed that the right standing of any person before God is realized exclusively by His sovereign grace. This divine work in the salvation of ruined sinners began in eternity past with the electing will of God, is carried out within time, and will be completed in eternity future. From start to finish, salvation is entirely the work of God.

This teaching was a dramatic departure from the false gospel of the Roman Catholic Church, which emphasized what man must do in order to receive and retain salvation. The teaching of the pope placed salvation in the hands of the priests serving the Mass. Further, it was seemingly purchased in the sale of indulgences. It required pilgrimages to shrines, the worship of images, and the veneration of saints—all non-biblical standards. Wycliffe's message was a dramatic departure from the apostate teaching of Rome. He maintained the centrality of faith in the true gospel as taught in Scripture, that "we may enter into that straight gate, as Christ our Savior and all that follow Him have done."[29]

---

28 Vaughan, *Tracts and Treatises of John de Wycliffe*, 17.
29 Ibid., 273.

Unconditional Election

For Wycliffe, the work of God in salvation began with His sovereign election of individual sinners before time began. He wrote: "For no one except for the predestined and the sanctified . . . is a member of the Church."[30] Those "predestined" are identified in this world as those who are being "sanctified." He understood that predestination before time and sanctification within time are inseparably bound together.

Wycliffe wrote that those who are predestined to salvation are true believers and, thus, comprise the true church: "Although the church is spoken of in many ways throughout Scripture, I think that we can conceive of it in its best known sense, namely the congregation of all the predestined."[31] Wycliffe believed the true church is made of those sovereignly chosen by God before the foundation of the world.

Absolute Predestination

Rejecting the Semi-Pelagian position that foreordination is merely divine foresight, Wycliffe affirmed that election is not based on any foreseen goodness in the one chosen. He writes: "Predestination is God's chief gift most freely given, since no one can merit his own predestination."[32] In his understanding, the cause for election lies entirely in God Himself, not

---

30 John Wycliffe, *De Ecclesia*, 4, 84/29-85/3, quoted in Takashi Shogimen, "Wyclif's Ecclesiology and Political Thought," in *A Companion to John Wyclif*, vol. 4, ed. Ian Christopher Levy (Leiden, Netherlands: Brill, 2006), 224.

31 Ibid., 216.

32 Ibid., 223.

because of any good in the one chosen. The reason for this is quite simple. The Scripture declares, "There is none who does good, there is not even one" (Rom. 3:12). If foreknowledge is merely foresight—which it cannot be—all God would see is no good in any person.

Wycliffe believed that the election of God is entirely by grace, not as a result of any admirable choices or good works by man. Nor is God's sovereign activity in salvation synergistic—that is, by grace and works. Rather, Wycliffe claimed it is monergistic, solely initiated and enacted by the electing grace of God. This weighty truth, he taught, should cause human hearts to fear God as they were created to do.

Initial Causality

Wycliffe taught that the exercise of the sovereign will of God in eternity past is the sole initiating cause in salvation. This began with His free choice of undeserving sinners before the foundation of the world. In matters of saving grace, he succinctly stated, "God is the first cause."[33] In other words, the first cause in salvation is not that God merely looks into the future to see which people will choose Christ, then chooses them. For Wycliffe, that would turn salvation on its head. It would make man the initiating cause of his own salvation. Instead, he stated that God—and God alone—is the first cause in man's salvation.

---

33 Vaughan, *The Tracts and Treatises of John De Wycliffe*, 110.

Irresistible Grace

Wycliffe taught that at the appointed time, the sovereign work of God applies salvation to the elect. He wrote: "Lord Jesus, turn us to you, and we shall be turned! Heal us and then we shall be verily holy; for without grace and help from you, may no man be truly turned or healed."[34] In other words, no man can turn to Christ until he is turned by Him. Spiritually dead sinners must be made alive and turned by Christ to Himself if they are to believe.

Wycliffe reiterated this truth when he wrote: "The prophet speaks . . . of souls perfectly turning to God, saying . . . 'He shall draw my feet, that is my soul and my affections, out of the snare, and the net of the love of this world.'"[35] He attested that God must draw sinners to faith in Christ, otherwise they will never escape the snares of the world. He preached, "Man cannot reject God's election."[36] Those whom God has chosen will be irresistibly drawn to Christ.

Saving Faith

Once a person is turned to Christ, Wycliffe taught, "Faith is a gift of God; and so God gives it not to man, unless He gives it graciously."[37] He believed that no man can truly trust Jesus Christ until God grants saving faith. This ability to believe in

---

34 Ibid., 361.

35 Wycliffe, John, *Writings of the Reverend and Learned John Wickliff*, 98.

36 John Wycliffe, Sermon E12/15, quoted in *English Wycliffite Sermons*, vol. 4, eds. Pamela Gordon and Anne Hudson (Oxford, England: Clarendon, 1996), 58.

37 Vaughan, *Tracts and Treatises of John de Wycliffe*, 193.

Christ does not come from the sinner, but from God. Faith is the undeserved gift of God that must be given to the elect.

Wycliffe explained that faith is looking to Jesus Christ: "As a right-looking at the adder of brass saved the people from the venom of the adder, so a right-looking by full belief on Christ saves His people."[38] Wycliffe referenced the narrative recorded in Numbers 21, when the Israelites were bitten by venomous snakes. They were instructed that if they would look to a lifted-up bronze serpent, they would live. This was an early type or foreshadowing of Christ being lifted up on the cross. Those who would look to Him will be saved.

Loving Faith

Such saving faith, Wycliffe believed, includes love for God. This affection for God can only come from Him. He maintained: "No man can . . . love God, or be chaste, unless God give it to him."[39] On their own, unconverted men cannot love God. Wycliffe taught that only when the Holy Spirit grants this new affection for God can a man truly love Him and believe in His Son, Jesus Christ. This supreme love is a distinguishing mark of true faith in God.

Justifying Faith

Contrary to the teaching of Rome, Wycliffe believed in the doctrine of *sola fide*—justification by faith alone. He wrote,

---

38 C. Matthew McMahon and Therese B. McMahon, *Life and Times of John Wycliffe* (London: Religious Tract Society, 1884), 124.

39 Wycliffe, *Writings of the Reverend and Learned John Wickliff,* 119.

"Trust wholly in Christ; rely altogether on His sufferings; beware of seeking to be justified in any other way than by His righteousness."[40] This core truth of justification by faith apart from works would later flourish and be boldly proclaimed in the Reformation. John Laird Wilson affirmed that Wycliffe stood "in perfect harmony with the teaching of the later Reformation."[41] As Wycliffe wrote, "We are predestined, that we may obtain divine acceptance."[42] He believed that those predestined by the Father are certain to be brought to faith in Christ and have imputed to them the righteousness of God in Christ.

Preserving Grace

All those predestined by God for salvation, Wycliffe taught, are kept eternally secure by the grace of God. He wrote: "This grace, which is called the grace of predestination, with the charity of final perseverance, cannot by any means fail."[43] Using the metaphor of shepherding, he stated, "The sheep cannot be ravished from Christ: what He has ordained to bliss must be blessed."[44] By this strong affirmation, Wycliffe

40 Mark Galli and Ted Olsen, *131 Christians Everyone Should Know* (Nashville, Tenn.: B&H, 2010), 212.

41 John Laird Wilson, *John Wycliffe: Patriot and Reformer* (New York: Funk & Wagnalls, 1884), 234.

42 Margaret Coxe, *The Life of John Wycliffe*, vol. 4 (Columbus, Ohio: Whiting, 1840), 254.

43 Vaughan, *The Life and Opinions of John de Wycliffe*, vol. 2, 353.

44 John Wycliffe, Sermon 173/35, quoted in *English Wycliffite Sermons,* vol. 4, eds. Pamela Gordon and Anne Hudson (Oxford, England: Clarendon, 1996), 57.

asserted that no believer will ever fail to persevere into eternity in their union with Jesus Christ. Those saved by God through "predestination," he maintained, "cannot be lost, since it is the foundation of glorification."[45] Wycliffe affirmed again and again that saving grace is irrevocable.

Those who believe in Christ, Wycliffe maintained, will be kept safe throughout time and eternity. Drawing upon Jesus' parable in Luke 15, he preached that, "final perseverance is required,"[46] and that, "The prodigal son is the man ordained by God to bliss, who may err but will return."[47] This knowledge of the preserving grace of God would encourage men to live in the truth of God's Word. Wycliffe's preaching aroused the determination of those who heard him boldly preach saying, "The Christian should be prepared to lose life in defense of Christ's love and of the Christian faith; true men should be hardy in God's cause and be ready for martyrdom—martyrs are comforted to hazard their body for God's law, since their soul cannot be destroyed."[48] It was this truth, that "their

---

45 John Wycliffe, "Tracts and Treatises of John de Wycliffe, D.D. with Selections and Translations from his Manuscripts, and Latin Works. Edited for The Wycliffe Society, with an Introductory Memoir, by the Rev. Robert Vaughan, D.D.," Online Library of Liberty, accessed July 16, 2020, https://oll.libertyfund.org/titles/wyclife-tracts-and-treatises-of-john-de-wycliffe/simple.

46 John Wycliffe, Sermon 62/85, quoted in *English Wycliffite Sermons,* vol. 4, eds. Pamela Gordon and Anne Hudson (Oxford, England: Clarendon, 1996), 60.

47 John Wycliffe, Sermon 158/83, quoted in *English Wycliffite Sermons,* vol. 4, eds. Pamela Gordon and Anne Hudson (Oxford, England: Clarendon, 1996), 57.

48 John Wycliffe, Sermon 53/31, 69/123, 63/36, quoted in *English Wycliffite Sermons,* vol. 4, eds. Pamela Gordon and Anne Hudson (Oxford, England: Clarendon, 1996), 77.

soul cannot be destroyed," that emboldened believers to make every heroic sacrifice for Christ.

THE DOCTRINE OF SANCTIFICATION

Wycliffe never confined his theology to ivory towers, but emphasized practical theology in all of the Christian's life. Though he was a man of the academy, he was also a man of the marketplace. He understood the ills of the people and the brokenness of society in England to be a direct result of the Fall and man's sinful condition. Having tasted the goodness of God in salvation, Wycliffe held that a believer's life must necessarily be changed by the Holy Spirit working through God's Word. To that end, Wycliffe was just as eminently and prolifically a practical theologian as an academic one.

Progressive Sanctification

Wycliffe understood that all those who are brought to faith in Jesus Christ also begin the lifelong process of being sanctified. Wycliffe writes, "God makes sinful man and unkind man, a good man; and all the goodness of this comes of the goodness of God."[49] Conversion, he believed, begins the miraculous change of a person's life. This is the sanctifying work of God's grace that produces the character of Jesus Christ in the one who believes. As quoted earlier, Wycliffe believed that "the

---

49 Wycliffe, *Writings of the Reverend and Learned John Wickliff*, 190.

predestined and the sanctified"[50] are inseparably connected. All the elect will surely be sanctified.

Genuine Worship

While the worship of Rome had been relegated to empty ritualistic formalism, Wycliffe saw the fruitful Christian life as consisting of vital worship in every facet of existence. He wrote in *A Short Rule of Life*:

> Think . . . how God hath saved thee from death and other mischief, and suffered many thousands to be lost that night, some in water, some in fire, and some by sudden death; and some to be damned without end. And for this goodness and mercy thank thy God with all thine heart. And pray Him to give thee grace to spend in that day, and evermore, all the powers of thy soul, as mind, understanding, reason, and will; and all the powers of thy body, as strength, beauty, and thy five senses, in His service and worship, and in nothing against His commandments; but in ready performance of His works of mercy, and to give good example of holy life, both in word and deed, to all men about thee.[51]

---

50 John Wycliffe, *De Ecclesia*, 4, 84/29-85/3, quoted in Takashi Shogimen, "Wyclif's Ecclesiology and Political Thought," in *A Companion to John Wyclif*, vol. 4, ed. Ian Christopher Levy (Leiden, Netherlands: Brill, 2006), 224.

51 John Wycliffe, *A Short Rule of Life*, quoted in Robert Vaughan, *Tracts and Treatises of John de Wycliffe* (London: Blackburn & Pardon, 1845), 47.

Instead of revering liturgies steeped in idolatry, Wycliffe emphasized a philosophy of the Christian life as a daily walk of communion with God. He recognized that God is involved in every facet of a believer's life. He saw every step of obedience to God as an offering of worship unto Him.

Godly Discipline

Wycliffe believed that Christians should honor God through a disciplined life in the pursuit of godliness. He exhorted his followers: "Look afterward that thou be well occupied, and no time idle, for the danger of temptation. Take meat and drink in measure, not too costly nor too lickerous, and be not too curious thereabout. But such as God sendeth thee with health, take it in such measure that thou be fresher in mind and understanding to serve God. And always thank Him for such gifts."[52]

As with his other writings, Wycliffe highlighted the necessity of gratitude to God for His richly bestowed gifts. He viewed all of life as a stewardship to honor God.

Reverential Awe

In Wycliffe's day, the church had created a system where the fear of God had been overshadowed by fear of man. For Wycliffe, this was an abdication of the most fundamental Christian responsibility. He exhorted priests and laymen alike:

---

52 Ibid., 47.

"Most of all fear God and His wrath; and most of all love God and His law, and His worship; and ask not principally for worldly reward, but in all thine heart desire the bliss of heaven in mercy of God, and thine own good life; and think much of the dreadful doom of pains of hell, to keep thee out of sin; and on the endless great joys of heaven, to keep thee in virtuous life; and according to thy skill teach others the same doing."[53]

Wycliffe taught that all believers must live with this sense of accountability before God. This fear of God comes from a profound sense of the holiness of God and the heinous nature of sin in one's own heart. The pervasive presence and acceptance of sinful living, especially prevalent among the clergy, Wycliffe believed, was an affront to God.

Fervent Prayer

Wycliffe taught the importance of the believer cultivating a devotional relationship with God. This personal communion with God sustained him through the heavy burdens of working towards true reformation. Prayer was the lifeline of Wycliffe's commitment to pursue God's cause. He wrote in his simple tract entitled *Prayer*, "Whoever liveth best, he prayeth best."[54] Wycliffe urged the practice of dependence upon God in prayer.

As believers are surrounded by many spiritual attacks, Wycliffe maintained the necessity of a life devoted to God in prayer, "Then Christian people shall have victory over the

---

53 Ibid.
54 Wycliffe, *Writings of the Reverend and Learned John Wickliff*, 142.

devil and cursed sin, then shall rest, and peace, and charity, dwell among them."[55] He understood that prayer was absolutely essential to living in spiritual victory over the forces of darkness.

In like manner, the opposite was also true. Should those professing to belong to God abandon their intimate fellowship with Him through prayer, they would cut themselves off from their source of spiritual power. Wycliffe wrote: "And if priests cease this holy life and good example, and this desire of righteousness, then Christian people shall be much overcome by sin, and have pestilence and wars, and woe enough; and unless God help, more endless woe in hell."[56]

The power of prayer, Wycliffe taught, must be guided by Scripture, especially as taught by Christ Himself: "but we ask in the name of Jesus, when we ask anything needful or profitable for the saving of men's souls, so that we ask this devoutly, of great desire, and wisely or humbly and lastingly, by firm faith, true hope and lasting charity, and whatever we ask thus, we shall have of the Father of heaven."[57]

Wycliffe was committed to the conviction that approaching the throne of grace enables believers to receive from the hands of the Lord what is needed to live their Christian lives.

---

55 Ibid.

56 Vaughan, "Tracts and Treatises of John de Wycliffe, D.D. with Selections and Translations from his Manuscripts, and Latin Works. Edited for The Wycliffe Society, with an Introductory Memoir, by the Rev. Robert Vaughan, D.D.," Online Library of Liberty, accessed July 16, 2020, https://oll.libertyfund.org/titles/wyclife -tracts-and-treatises-of-john-de-wycliffe/simple.

57 Wycliffe, *Writings of the Reverend and Learned John Wickliff*, 143.

The Doctrine of the Church

While Rome contended that salvation was found in the church, Wycliffe maintained that it is found in Christ alone. This stance was a dramatic departure from what was being taught by the priests throughout England. A person can be in the church, Wycliffe contended, but not be found in saving union with Christ. Such a person, though inside the walls of the church, is outside of salvation. Only those in Christ possess a right standing before God. In Wycliffe's view, these true believers alone constituted the true church.

Visible and Invisible Church

Wycliffe believed that those claiming membership in the church are not necessarily true believers in Jesus Christ. Wycliffe held that the visible church is composed of both the elect and the non-elect, a mixed congregation of both believers and unbelievers. He knew this was certainly the case with the Roman Catholic Church, which contained both wheat and tares.

Wycliffe taught that the true church is the invisible church—made up exclusively of those believers who were predestined by God unto eternal life. To this pre-Reformer, the invisible church was composed of the total number of the elect. It is said that he "viewed the church as the community of the elect."[58] This emphasis on the church as the fellowship

---

58 "Predestination," Biblical Training, accessed July 16, 2020, https://www.biblicaltraining.org/library/predestination.

of elect believers repeatedly appears in his writings. Wycliffe refuted the false claims made by Rome that salvation is found in the church. He recognized the fact that believers and unbelievers alike participate in the visible church. To the contrary, the invisible church represents the true body of Christ, those regenerated by His Spirit.

Divine Head

Further, Wycliffe maintained that Jesus Christ is the sole head of the church. No human leader—not even the pontiff of Rome—can claim to be the head of the church on earth. Sovereign headship belongs to Christ alone. At the right hand of the Father, Jesus rules over all things as Lord of the entire universe. This includes the church. By the Father's decree, the highest authority over the church belongs exclusively to Christ. Wycliffe wrote, "Christ is the supreme Lord, while the pope is a man, and liable to mortal sin, and who while in mortal sin, according to divines, is unfitted for dominion."[59] Christ reigns and, therefore, His authority is final. Such unquestionable power does not belong to the pope, priests, or other human church leaders.

H.B. Workman explains the Oxford professor's position: "The church, as the mystical body of the predestinated, is a unity that knows nothing of papal primacies and hierarchies, and of the 'sects' of monks, friars, and priests; nor can the

---

59 Wycliffe, *Writings of the Reverend and Learned John Wickliff*, 14.

salvation of the elect be conditioned by masses, indulgences, penance, or other devices of sacerdotalism."[60]

Wycliffe's position stripped the church hierarchies of his day of their self-claimed power to preside over the body of Christ. Instead, the right to rule the church could only come from Christ alone.

False Leaders

Wycliffe saw nothing in Scripture to support the false invention of the papacy. Nor did he see any need for its existence. He viewed all popes as the Antichrist because of their blatant betrayal of Scripture and corruption of the gospel. In Wycliffe's view, the pope is only the bishop of one local church in Rome. In fact, the bishop of Rome could be outside the saving grace of Christ as a reprobate. All popes, cardinals, and priests, Wycliffe stated, are not among the elect merely by virtue of their role. He called the monastic orders false "sects" and monks "the pests of society," "the enemies of religion," and "the promoters of every crime."[61] He believed that the preaching of the friars was devoid of Scripture and entirely hypocritical.

From rebuking the local friars to the Vatican, Wycliffe minced no words, "The greater part of the clergy is heretical and the highest are the worst."[62] In other words, the higher

---

60 *The London Quarterly Review* 95 (1901): 264.

61 *Life and Times of John Wycliffe* (London: Religious Tract Society, 1884), 40.

62 John Wycliffe, *De Semonia*, eds. Michael Henry Dziewicki and Sigmund Herzberg-Fränkel (United Kingdom: Wyclif Society, 1966), 4.

these men rose in the ecclesiastical hierarchy of Rome, the more corrupt they became. He viewed with open eyes the defiling effect of these man-made offices upon the doctrinal and moral purity of the true Church. New leaders, rooted in Scripture and the Holy Spirit, were needed.

THE DOCTRINE OF LAST THINGS

Like Christians in every age, Wycliffe was a man who wrestled to define the end of time. Throughout his writings and sermons he appeared to have great concern over the last days and how that culmination would manifest itself. He can be regarded in some ways as orthodox by contemporary Christians in certain areas, and confused or even unorthodox, in others. His holding fast to apostolic teaching on cardinal truths in some areas did not guarantee perfection of belief in all areas.

Heaven and Hell

An orthodox belief in Heaven and Hell were a catalyst for Wycliffe and his evangelistic zeal. The reality of these two eternal places were certain in his thinking and served as central to all other beliefs about the age to come. He wrote of the end goal of sound theology and preaching by saying, "The goal of theology rests in that clear vision of the Trinity. . . . Surely it is more effective in preparing one for the journey homeward [to Heaven] with respect to faith, hope, and love."[63] It was for this eternal reality that right theology prepared the believer. He described in his work *De Ecclesia Dominio* the church's existence with Christ in glory. He said, "The first part is in bliss with Christ, the head of the church, and containeth angels and blessed men that now be in heaven."[64] By this we know that Wycliffe held to this fundamental truth regarding the end of time and eternity.

On the other hand, Wycliffe warned against the pastoral malpractice of distorting the gospel, that would result in the hearer being condemned to Hell. He wrote, "Now it is clear that the spiritual pastures through which one ought to drive the Lord's flock are truths of Scripture . . . and not the path which leads to hell."[65] This realization fired the red-hot preaching of the gospel by Wycliffe and his unyielding polemics against the church's heresy in his day. Utilizing the imagery of a sounding trumpet as the "organ of the Bridegroom's voice" in Revelation, he stated, "Just like the Sons of Thunder, he should courageously preach sermons of great authority."[66] So strong was Wycliffe's belief in a literal hell that he was

---

63 John Wycliffe, *On the Truth of Holy Scripture*, trans. Ian Christopher Levy, in *John Wycliffe on the Truth of Holy Scripture* (Kalamazoo, Mich.: Medieval Institute Publications, 2001), 278.

64 John Wycliffe, *De Ecclesia Dominio*, quoted in Robert Vaughan, *Tracts and Treatises of John de Wycliffe*, 74.

65 John Wycliffe, *On the Truth of Holy Scripture*, trans. Ian Christopher Levy, in *John Wycliffe on the Truth of Holy Scripture* (Kalamazoo, Mich.: Medieval Institute Publications, 2001), 289.

66 John Wycliffe, *On the Truth of Holy Scripture*, trans. Ian Christopher Levy, in *John Wycliffe on the Truth of Holy Scripture* (Kalamazoo, Mich.: Medieval Institute Publications, 2001), 282.

willing to defy every established authority and tradition, so that men's souls might be saved regardless of personal cost.

Purgatory

John Wycliffe was not only a man for his time, he was a man of his time. Unfortunately, he retained some error in his thinking, shaped in part by a lifetime under the doctrines of the Roman Catholic Church. Like the vast majority of others in his day, a belief in a purgatory of some kind was a presumed conclusion. Scholars have, however, been quick to point out Wycliffe's view of purgatory was divergent from mainstream thought even in his day. Writing in *De Ecclesia Dominio,* he stated his belief that a second place in which the church resided was a purgatory, awaiting a final purification of sin and subsequent promotion to heaven. He wrote, "The second part of the church be saints in purgatory, and these sin not-anew, but purge their old sins."[67] Though diverging from what the Reformers would later clarify as the Bible's teaching on this matter and the denial of an existence of purgatory, Wycliffe lived his life in the murky pre-dawn light of the Reformation to come.

EVANGELICAL ORTHODOXY

The evangelical theology of Wycliffe was the real power that energized his ministry. In his faithful devotion to Christ, he

---

67 John Wycliffe, *De Ecclesia Dominio*, quoted in Robert Vaughan, *Tracts and Treatises of John de Wycliffe*, 74.

left a great mark upon the church that had gone far adrift. His sound doctrine was the driving force of his preaching, teaching, and writing that began a new movement in his day. In Wycliffe's ministry, we observe the explosive power of the gospel truth when it is proclaimed in the power of the Holy Spirit. Though it would be another one hundred and fifty years before the Reformation would come, Wycliffe was a forerunner who laid in place the key doctrines upon which the Reformers would build their history-altering movement.

The church in the centuries that followed Wycliffe owed much to the heroic labors of this valiant theologian. His work was not a shallow effort, but one built upon the sturdy footing of sound doctrine. May such rock-solid truths support and carry our own labors, founded upon the Word of God.

CHAPTER FOUR

Bible
Scholar

*Wycliffe was beyond dispute the most eminent scholar
who taught for any length of time at Oxford.*[1]

—PHILIP SCHAFF

L ike the Reformers who followed John Wycliffe, this
renowned professor and scholar possessed a brilliant mind
and towering intellect. He had been trained at the highest
level in the leading academic institution in the nation—
Oxford University. After Wycliffe graduated, he joined the
faculty there and taught philosophy and theology for many
years. Throughout his entire adult life, he mastered his subject
matter in this highly-esteemed university. Wycliffe came to be
recognized as an outstanding intellectual force in England. In

---

1   Philip Schaff, *History of the Christian Church*, vol. 6, *The Middle Ages* (Peabody,
Mass.: Hendrickson, 2006), 326.

75

his day, many even considered Wycliffe to be the leading mind in Europe.

Wycliffe was profoundly influenced by studying the greatest thinkers of past centuries. This broad-reaching exposure sharpened his understanding of philosophical worldviews and theological systems. Wycliffe had great familiarity with many of the early church fathers, including the Latin church leaders: Jerome, Ambrose, Augustine, and Gregory.[2] This interaction with the brightest minds in theology from previous centuries gave Wycliffe a strategic grasp in many realms of profound thought. He was even well-versed in matters of legal jurisprudence.[3] Whether it was in theology, philosophy, or civil law, Wycliffe became a torchbearer for substantial reform in the church and the nation.

A STALWART FORERUNNER

The fourteenth century proved to be a pivotal period at Oxford. Though many of the great Scholastics at the school had been followers of Augustinian thought, William of Ockham was influential in reviving Pelagianism through his lectures. He implied that fallen man could earn God's grace, meriting salvation through his moral abilities. While scholars who write about Ockham refer to his views as

---

2   John Wycliffe, *Writings of the Reverend and Learned John Wickliff* (London: The Religious Tract Society, 1831), 11.

3   Ibid.

semi-Pelagianism, his theological system was actually more closely aligned with Pelagianism, with its emphasis on the power of the human will to achieve grace. Eventually, Pope John XXII summoned William to Avignon in southern France to answer heresy charges.

Amid this Pelagian revival, God raised up a stalwart of Augustinianism to champion the cause of sovereign grace. His name was Thomas Bradwardine (1290–1349). As both a student and professor at Oxford, Bradwardine confronted the teaching of William of Ockham's Pelagian views at the school. As a result, a revival of Augustinianism burst forth in the third decade of the fourteenth century.[4]

Bradwardine served a strategic role in church history. His life paved the way for the resurgence of the doctrine of predestination in the years leading up to the Reformation.[5] He helped shape the convictions of John Wycliffe, who was considered to be the first pre-Reformer. Justo L. González notes, "On the doctrine of predestination, Wycliffe seems to have read Augustine through the eyes of Bradwardine." Thus, the reformational preaching of Wycliffe can be directly traced back to Bradwardine, who received his teaching from Augustine.[6]

---

4   J.V. Fesko, *Diversity within the Reformed Tradition: Supra- and Infralapsarianism in Calvin, Dort, and Westminster* (Greenville, S.C.: Reformed Academic, 2001), 40.

5   R.E.D. Clark, "Thomas Bradwardine," in *New International Dictionary of the Christian Church*, gen. ed. J.D. Douglas (Grand Rapids, Mich.: Zondervan, 1978), 798.

6   Justo L. Gonzalez, *A History of Christian Thought*, vol. 2, *From Augustine to the Eve of the Reformation* (Nashville, Tenn.: Abingdon, 1971), 326.

It was into this doctrinal battle that Wycliffe was thrust in the second half of the fourteenth century. By Wycliffe's day, Rome had again contrived a scheme of works-based salvation that appeared to be turning the tide back to Pelagianism.

FIGHTING THE GOOD FIGHT

In Wycliffe's major works, he presented and defended arguments with profound clarity. This was especially true in his polemic writings against the heresies of the church of Rome. With pen in hand, Wycliffe earnestly contended for the truth. As Wycliffe fought the good fight for the pure gospel, his writings were a powerful force against the deceptive errors in the arena of public controversy. So prolific was Wycliffe's intellectual genius and immense productivity that he often wrote more than one treatise on a given subject. It was not uncommon for him to address the same topic from multiple approaches.

Although Wycliffe is a significant figure in church history, his writings are tragically neglected today. Matthew Spinka writes in *Advocates of Reform*, "As is generally known, Wycliffe's writings are both linguistically and stylistically exceedingly involved and difficult."[7] Because of the density in content, few have taken up the challenge of translating and abridging even Wycliffe's most seminal works. It took the formidable scholar

---

7   Matthew Spinka, *Advocates of Reform: From Wyclif to Erasmus* (Louisville, Ky.: Westminster John Knox, 2006), 25.

Ford Lewis Battles, most well-known for his translation of Calvin's *Institutes*, to more recently translate Wycliffe's *On the Pastoral Office* from Latin into English.[8]

Many of Wycliffe's writings are preserved in either fragmentary or whole form in libraries and universities across the United Kingdom and Ireland. The Religious Tract Society in London estimates that more than 300 of his sermons have also survived and been preserved in some form.[9] Several of the works mentioned in this chapter are contained in Wycliffe's larger doctrinal volume, *Summa Theologica*, and represent the heart of his literary contributions.

ON DIVINE DOMINION (1373–1374)

A vital aspect of Wycliffe's polemical writings was his views on the relationship between church and state. In *On Divine Dominion* (*De Dominio Divino*, 1373–1374), he attacked the papal authority on the grounds that such an office is nowhere found in the Bible. He could find no scriptural support for the pope's political and national intrusions. In fact, he stated that the papacy is in direct opposition to the supreme authority of Scripture. Worse, the office of the pope obscures the church's true authority—which must be found exclusively in the Bible.

---

8   Ibid.
9   Wycliffe, *Writings of the Reverend and Learned John Wickliff*, 184.

Inordinate Wealth

The most visible manifestation of Rome's overreach in Wycliffe's day was the inordinate accumulation of wealth and legal immunity gained by the church and its clergy. Because God's Word had been diluted by extrabiblical methods, unjust practices abounded without any confrontation or correction by Scripture. In response, Wycliffe opened *On Divine Dominion* by stating, "Since false glosses make God's law dark, and hinder secular men to sustain and keep it, of such false glosses should each man be aware."[10] Wycliffe believed that the king of England should remove Rome's accumulation of excessive wealth and vast property holdings.

Stephen Lahey comments, "Because Wycliffe saw the fourteenth-century church enjoying the lion's share of property ownership in England, he argued that the king was bound by God to relieve the church of its property, and to rule over it as a divinely-appointed steward."[11] As Wycliffe saw it, the church in England, under the dominion of Rome, had become inordinately worldly and had forsaken its primary mission of preaching the Word of God.

Wycliffe's chief concern was that the spiritual health of

---

10 Wycliffe, "Tracts and Treatises of John de Wycliffe, D.D. with Selections and Translations from his Manuscripts, and Latin Works. Edited for The Wycliffe Society, with an Introductory Memoir, by the Rev. Robert Vaughan, D.D.," Online Library of Liberty, accessed April 5, 2020, https://oll.libertyfund.org/titles/1838#Wycliffe_0882_491.

11 Stephen Lahey, "John Wyclif's Political Philosophy," *The Stanford Encyclopedia of Philosophy* (Spring 2014 Edition), ed. Edward N. Zalta, accessed April 5, 2020, https://plato.stanford.edu/archives/spr2014/entries/wyclif-political/.

the church was hindered by its enormous endowments of ostentatious wealth. He saw the church devolving into being a worldly landlord, acting oppressively against those for whom it was charged to care. He said, "This endowing against God's law, doeth harm to lords, and clerks, and commons, both bodily harm, and harm in their souls."[12] In short, Wycliffe believed the higher authority of Scripture must be recovered and restored to its rightful place. Otherwise, the church would remain captive to its worldly desires and fail to fulfill its ministry and calling.

On Civil Dominion (1375–1376)

In his treatise, *On Civil Dominion* (*De Civili Dominio*), Wycliffe confronted the Roman Catholic Church's arrogant assertion of its authority over the English crown and nobility. He believed that England was under no obligation to support a corrupt church, especially one so ungodly and greedy for power. If a spiritual or secular leader is faithless before God, Wycliffe maintained he may be stripped of his office and privileges. He wrote, "Men hold whatever they have received from God as stewards, and if found faithless could justly be

---

12 Wycliffe, "Tracts and Treatises of John de Wycliffe, D.D. with Selections and Translations from his Manuscripts, and Latin Works. Edited for The Wycliffe Society, with an Introductory Memoir, by the Rev. Robert Vaughan, D.D.," Online Library of Liberty, accessed April 5, 2020, https://oll.libertyfund.org/titles/1838#Wycliffe _0882_491.

deprived of it."[13] He insisted nothing belongs to man, who is a mere steward of God's possessions. Everything ultimately belongs to God and must be used according to His desires.

Improper Authority

Appealing to the witness of Scripture, Wycliffe stated, "Earthly power should only be given to the righteous and not to the sinner."[14] He explained, "If through transgression a man forfeited his [eternal] privileges, then of necessity his temporal possessions were also lost."[15] Thus, Wycliffe maintained that wicked rulers have no legitimate authority with which they rule. If the power they hold is therefore unjustly kept and unlawfully exercised, it may be taken from them.

In this work, Wycliffe writes:

If it be said that God has invested the priest with authority over the lay world, let it be answered from the teaching of Christ and his apostles that the priest is not to be the master of the flock, but their minister. He has received his office not to rule, but to preach and interpret the word of God. Civil dominion has

---

13 John Wycliffe, quoted in Samuel Parkes Cadman, *The Three Religious Leaders of Oxford and Their Movements: John Wycliffe, John Wesley, John Henry Newman* (United States: Macmillan, 1916), 66.

14 John Wycliffe, *De Veritate Sacrae Scriptura*.

15 John Wycliffe, "De Civili Dominio," quoted in Donald L. Roberts, "John Wycliffe and the Dawn of the Reformation" *Christian History Magazine* no. 3 (1983), accessed April 5, 2020, https://christianhistoryinstitute.org/magazine/article/john -wycliffe-and-the-dawn-of-the-reformation.

not been granted to the priest; spiritual dominion, however, may be granted to every faithful layman, and every Christian may be priest and king.

God's Law is sufficient also for the secular government, so that neither a civil nor a papal code of law is needed. In the Divine Law, the King has a standard for all secular affairs, whether he wishes to reward its defenders or to punish its enemies.[16]

Here, Wycliffe draws a line between ruling and shepherding in the church. He affirms that the role of clergy is to care for their congregation, not rule over them in tyranny. The priest was not assigned by God to be domineering in civil or spiritual affairs. This perspective was in total contradiction to what was being practiced in Wycliffe's time—and must be corrected.

THE TRUTH OF HOLY SCRIPTURE (1378)

When Wycliffe returned to Oxford in 1378, he knew he must uphold the Bible as the sole criterion for determining what the church must believe. He was convinced that these two subjects—what the Bible teaches and what the church believes—were to be inseparably bound together. In turn, what the church believes will determine how the church perceives

---

16 John Wycliffe, *On Civil Dominion.*

itself and how it conducts itself. Following his treatment of the pope and church's authority, specifically in regard to the ownership of property, he wrote *The Truth of Holy Scripture*, as Book VI in the *Summa Theologica*. This book would become foundational to his following twelve books, comprising his theological magnum opus.

In *The Truth of Holy Scripture* (*De Veritate Sacrae Scripturae*), Wycliffe made the bold assertion that the Bible is the sole standard for Christian doctrine. Parker explains that Wycliffe "came to stress with growing emphasis that God's word, the Bible, was the final and only justification for any conclusion."[17] The Bible, Wycliffe argued, must hold preeminence over the teachings of the church fathers, ecclesiastical councils, church tradition, and even the pope himself.

Preeminent Scripture

In addition, Wycliffe stated that the Scripture contains all that is necessary for salvation, without the addition of human inventions. He believed that all people, not merely the priests, should read Scripture for themselves. Accordingly, he insisted that a translation of the Bible in the English language should be made available to the people. This stance was a radical departure from the ruling of the Council of Toulouse (1229), which strictly forbade the laity to read the Bible. According to Roman Catholic law, translating the Bible into a common

---

17 G.H.W. Parker, *The Morningstar: Wycliffe and the Dawn of the Reformation* (Grand Rapids, Mich.: Eerdmans, 1965), 42.

language was a heresy punishable by death. This was a sinister strategy to keep spiritual power solely in the hands of the pope and the leaders under his control.

Church historian Dr. Nick Needham comments on what Wycliffe wrote in this work concerning the Bible: "He published a book called *The Truth of Holy Scripture*, in which he argued that the Bible was the only source of Christian doctrine, by which believers must test all the teachings of the church, including the early church fathers, the papacy and ecumenical councils. All Christians should read the Bible, so it must be translated from the Latin of the Vulgate into the native languages of the various nations."[18]

This appeal to Scripture would be the vital heartbeat of Wycliffe's ministry. He wholeheartedly believed that the Bible must be made available to all English-speaking people if they are to know it and follow its truths.

Needham further describes Wycliffe's views on the Bible: "Wycliffe's views here were quite revolutionary. In the Middle Ages in Western Europe, people had come to regard the Bible as the clergy's book. Priests and theologians alone could interpret it correctly and teach laypeople what it meant. The Catholic church looked with great suspicion, even outright hostility, on the idea that a layperson should study the Bible for himself."[19]

---

18 Needham, *2000 Years of Christ's Power*, vol. 2 (Fearn, Ross-shire, Scotland: Christian Focus, 2015), 415.

19 Ibid.

Wycliffe's conviction to translate the Bible into the common language of the English people was growing. This desire was fueled by his burning passion to see students, congregants, and fellow citizens flourish in the knowledge of God's Word.

ON THE CHURCH (1378)

Wycliffe advanced his argument yet further against the pope and the church in Rome when he wrote *On the Church* (*De Ecclesia*) in 1378. In this watershed work, Wycliffe identified the true church not by its organizational structure, nor by its number of worshipers in attendance. In Wycliffe's understanding, the pope and the clergy were subject to the authority of Scripture. Accordingly, the church was to be governed in all of its life and conduct according to the principles of holy truth contained in the Bible.

As noted earlier in chapter 3, Wycliffe wrote that the true church of God is the total number of the elect. In this conviction, he stood in agreement with the luminary theologian Augustine of Hippo, who made the same distinction between the visible and invisible church. Wycliffe stressed that one can be in the visible church and participate in its rituals, but not be in the true body of Christ. Therefore, a mere church attender with an empty profession of Christ is without a right standing before God.

Wycliffe stressed that salvation belongs exclusively to those who are predestined by God to eternal life. This standing comes through the sovereign grace of God alone, not through human activity in church membership or any outward efforts to please God.

The True Body of Christ

Wycliffe emphatically stated that the true church was composed of the "congregation of the predestined."[20] Of the real body of Christ, he wrote, "Neither place nor human election makes a person a member of the Church, but divine predestination in respect of whoever with perseverance follows Christ in love, and in abandoning all his worldly goods suffers to defend His law."[21] Such beliefs were scandalous in their strong denunciation of the teaching of Rome.

Creating further controversy, Wycliffe maintained that Jesus Christ is the only head of the church. His statement was pointed, intended to criticize the pope in Rome. Wycliffe contended that the pope is, at most, only the subordinate shepherd of one visible, local church in Rome. He maintained that Jesus Christ is the only sovereign head over the true church around the world, which is composed of the elect only. Those chosen by the Father before the foundation of the world will be irresistibly called by the Holy Spirit into communion with Jesus Christ. These alone constitute the true body of Christ.

---

20 *De Ecclesia*, ed. J. Loserth (London, 1886), 1.

21 Ibid., 76.

Radical Conviction

These doctrinal convictions were nothing short of revolutionary and further escalated the building conflict between the church in Rome and Wycliffe. Regarding the pope, Wycliffe stated: "If he is predestined and exercises his pastoral office, [he] is the head of as much of the church militant as he governs, so that if he thus rules preeminently the whole of the church militant according to Christ's law, then he is the particular head of it under the Supreme Head, Jesus Christ."[22]

Wycliffe's radical teaching on the church and his rejection of the pope's claim to be supreme head of the church were intensified by the historical event known as the Papal Schism. Beginning in 1378, two men became locked in a heated conflict, both staking their claim to be "head of the church." Pope Gregory XI had returned to Rome to rule from the Vatican, but Clement VII claimed the papal throne's authority rested on him in Avignon, France. Wycliffe used this heated dispute to disprove the legitimacy of the chief office of the pope. He wrote in his tract:

> [T]he apostles of Christ filled the world with God's grace. But long after . . . [the] priest of Rome . . . brought in a new guile, and moved the emperor of Rome to endow his church. When the life of the priest was thus changed, his name was changed. He was not

---

22 Ibid., 19.

called the apostle, or the disciple of Christ, but he was called the pope, and head of all [the] holy church: and afterwards came other names, by the feigning of hypocrites, so that some say he is even [ruling] with . . . Christ, and highest vicar of Christ, to do on earth whatever he likes; and some flourish other names and say that he is most blessed father. . . . [M]alice is stronger when it is gathered in one person, and it is of less strength when it is dispersed among many. . . . [P]opes . . . are Antichrists. If they say that Christ's church must have a head here on earth, true it is, for Christ is the head.[23]

THE PASTORAL OFFICE (1378)

In another book, *The Pastoral Office* (1378), Wycliffe confronted the unfaithful clergy he saw defaming the church by their carnal worldliness. He stressed that all those in the ministry should live godly lives, something he perceived was sorely missing in the spiritual leaders of his day. These men should model the message they declare from the Word of God, not contradict it. They must demonstrate godly lives of humble obedience to Scripture, setting an example that can be clearly seen by all.

---

23 Wycliffe, "Tracts and Treatises of John de Wycliffe, D.D. with Selections and Translations from his Manuscripts, and Latin Works. Edited for The Wycliffe Society, with an Introductory Memoir, by the Rev. Robert Vaughan, D.D.," Online Library of Liberty, accessed April 5, 2020, https://oll.libertyfund.org/titles/1838#Wycliffe _0882_528.

Wycliffe further lamented the deficiency of true preaching in the church by the priests. As he examined the earthly ministry of Jesus Christ, Wycliffe noted that gospel preaching was His main ministry. The minister's highest service, therefore, is found in the preaching of the Word. Biblical exposition, he said, holds greater importance than administering the sacraments. When the Word is preached, sinners are effectively converted and the church is most spiritually strengthened.

THE POWER OF THE POPE (1379)

Driving a greater wedge between Rome and himself, Wycliffe wrote *The Power of the Pope* (*De Potestate Papae*) in 1379. In this polemic work, he continued to assert that the papal office was purely a man-made fabrication and not an institution established by God. He stressed that any pope who did not lead a godly life and hold to the gospel teaching of Christ was an apostate. In fact, he claimed that a worldly pope is the Antichrist himself. These accusations were fierce and unbridled. Wycliffe would later escalate this charge and maintain that all popes, regardless of their lifestyle, are antichrists.

His reasoning for such a bold assertion stemmed from his belief that the pope's dictates directly contradict the authority of Scripture: "Forasmuch as through his decrees God's commands, by his commandments Christ's commandments, by his decretals Paul's epistles, by his canon law the canonical scripture, was vilified, nullified, utterly defaced and debased."[24] For this reason, Wycliffe declared the Pope to be, "most especially antichrist."[25] For Wycliffe, Scripture necessitates a zero-tolerance conviction for anything added to or taken away from God's Word. As the church in Rome based most of its spiritual activity in extrabiblical tradition, Wycliffe condemned their practices, saying they added to the Scriptures. This, he contended, was defying the divine mandate to submit to the Bible.

Wycliffe's views were extraordinarily bold, and he believed that every layman should hold to them as well. Wherever the pope was found "to go contrary to Christ's laws,"[26] Wycliffe urged that even those "inferior might, and in conscience ought, not only to disobey him, but to reprove, correct, and contradict him."[27] By giving these directions, Wycliffe paved the way for a grassroots movement of common Christians to proclaim the Word of God that would be known as the Lollard movement. He empowered believers in his day to challenge the established traditions of the Roman Catholic Church that were not based upon Scripture. This movement was composed of the Lollards, who were armed with the truth of the Bible alone. Founded by Wycliffe, these men opposed

---

24 Wycliffe, *Writings of the Reverend and Learned John Wickliff* (United Kingdom: Religious Tract Society, 1831), 184.

25 Ibid.

26 Ibid.

27 Ibid.

the forces of Satan, chiefly personified in the corruption of the papacy.

On Apostasy (c. 1379, c. 1382)

Wycliffe next published *On Apostasy (De Apostasia)* between 1379 and 1382, which struck a devastating blow to the core doctrine of the church in Rome, their essential belief in the transubstantiation of the Mass. He completely refuted the validity of the Mass, bluntly denying that the bread and wine transform into the body and blood of Christ in the hands of the priest. Wycliffe firmly denounced the sacramental power of the priesthood and denied any efficacy in the Mass to remove sin. He opened this work with a cannon blast, saying, "Any act that loosens the bond of worship between man and the Father is a sin against the Father. The pope, when he has broken by heresy the bond of divine service, is no longer apostolic but apostate."[28] He argued that this false doctrine held by Rome was in blatant contradiction to Scripture.

Wycliffe also stated that transubstantiation was a recent novelty in doctrine, never taught by the early church. This fabrication, he claimed, was only recently promoted by the church starting in 1215 by the Fourth Lateran Council. Further, Wycliffe openly rejected all church rituals, ceremonies, and rites not specifically taught in the Bible. He believed these

---

28 John Wycliffe, *De Apostasia*, trans. Michael Henry Dziewicki (London: Wyclif Society, 1889), 40.

man-contrived external formalities do not help the worship of God, but actually hinder it. Later in church history, his belief in worship being regulated by Scripture came to be known as the "regulative principle."

ON THE EUCHARIST (1380)

Wycliffe was so adamantly opposed to the idolatry of the Mass that he wrote his next polemic, *On the Eucharist (De Eucharisto)*, in 1380 to again refute it. He staunchly objected to the blasphemous idea that the priest had the power to turn the bread and wine into the actual body and blood of Christ. At the Fourth Lateran Council, transubstantiation had been declared a dogma of faith, and it was stated that the priestly consecration of the elements transformed them into the real body and blood of Christ. Wycliffe completely rejected this thinking as the sin of idolatry—no small charge.

In *On The Eucharist*, Wycliffe wrote:

> When we see the host, we ought to believe not that it is itself the body of Christ, but that the body of Christ is sacramentally concealed in it. . . . We Christians are permitted to deny that the bread which we consecrate is identical with the body of Christ, although it is the efficacious sign of it. . . .
>
> [Those who identify them] fail to distinguish between the figure and the thing figured and to heed

the figurative meaning. . . . The spiritual receiving of the body of Christ consists not in bodily receiving, chewing, or touching of the consecrated host, but in the feeding of the soul out of the fruitful faith according to which our spirit is nourished in the Lord. . . . For nothing is more horrible than the necessity of eating the flesh carnally and of drinking the blood carnally of a man [Jesus Christ] loved so dearly.[29]

Not only was the teaching of the church errant, these critical sacraments of the bread and the cup, as well as baptism, had become a commodity with which to appease the rich, enrich the church, and abuse the poor. Against these flagrant abuses Wycliffe made his stand.

CONCLUSIONS (C. 1381)

In 1380, Wycliffe was attacked at Oxford for his previously published views that opposed the Mass. That same year, he appeared before a council summoned by the Chancellor of the University of Oxford, where he gave a defense of his controversial positions on this subject. Wycliffe's rebuttal came in the form of twelve stated conclusions. The next year, in May 1381, Wycliffe assembled a dozen theses into a document called *The Twelve Conclusions*, which defended and

---

29   John Wycliffe, *The Eucharist*, 1.2, 11; 7.58; 7.15.

expounded his staunch doctrinal position. This effort, though, only confirmed his beliefs as seemingly heretical in the eyes of his ecclesiastical and political opponents.

THE SEVEN HERESIES (C. 1381–C. 1384)

Sometime between 1381 and 1384, Wycliffe wrote another fiery polemic treatise entitled *The Seven Heresies*, in which he continued his onslaught against the false teaching of the Roman Catholic Church. In this exposing work, he used the Lord's Prayer as the basis for his aggressive attack upon Rome. From this model prayer given by Jesus Christ, Wycliffe addressed seven aspects of this prayer and showed how the church was grossly heretical in its teachings. Strategically, he used the Lord's Prayer because it was the one part of Scripture with which the laity was most familiar. He used this well-known passage which was so firmly held to and often repeated by the Roman Catholic Church to overtly condemn its deviant practices.

First, Wycliffe addressed the opening of the prayer, "Our Father, who is in heaven." At this point, he confronted Rome for its outrageous teaching that prayers offered to God the Father by priests were more effectual than prayers offered by any believer. Second, when considering "Your kingdom come," Wycliffe rebuked Rome for declaring "bad prelates"—meaning carnal priests—to be members of the kingdom of God by ecclesiastical rite rather than by saving faith in Jesus Christ. Third, in light of "Your will be done," he condemned the papacy for granting indulgences and claiming to impart salvation—practices he declared to be contrary to the will of God in Scripture. Roman Catholic teaching was overtly disobedient to the commands of Christ for the church to be the bulwark of truth and grace.

Pointed Criticism

Fourth, Wycliffe confronted Rome for its teaching on transubstantiation in light of the entreaty "give us this day our daily bread." He claimed that in the Mass the bread remained physical bread and that Jesus is not bodily present in the elements. Fifth, he rebuked the church in Rome for assuming it can grant absolution of sins, a right that belongs to God alone. He noted that the petition, "Forgive us our trespasses" is addressed directly to God, who alone can grant forgiveness, not to the priest. Sixth, Wycliffe refuted Rome for teaching that friars are granted an exemption from temptation. Instead, he maintained that Jesus urged all believers to pray, "lead us not into temptation." This included the friars. All those in Christ need the Holy Spirit to preserve them in purity of heart as they seek to follow Him.

Seventh, Wycliffe challenged Rome for teaching that monastic vows automatically protect priests from devilish assault. This is contrary to what Jesus instructed all saints—without exceptions—to pray "deliver us from evil." All seven of these Roman Catholic beliefs were directly confronted by Wycliffe as being in violation of the Lord's Prayer. He believed Rome stood contrary to Scripture and, therefore, in opposition to God.

OF PERFECT LIFE

Though the writings of Wycliffe often took a necessary polemic tone against the heresies and abuses of his day, he remained deeply concerned for the spiritual health of those professing to be Christians. As a professor and apologist, his pen flamed hot with the zeal of correction. But as a pastor and preacher, he pled earnestly for souls to be devoted to Christ in every arena of life. Henry Hervey Baber wrote that *Of Perfect Life*, alternately titled *Poor Caitiff*, was a "volume of small tracts, written in English, for the purpose of instructing the lower orders of the community in the most useful precepts of the Christian religion."[30] This was a work directed to the laity or the common people.

Based on Luke 9:23, *Of Perfect Life* was an instructive manual on discipleship. The tract began with these words, "Christ, not compelling, but freely counselling each man to perfect life, saith thus."[31] Against the backdrop of the self-righteous

---

30   Henry Hervey Baber, *The New Testament Translated from the Latin, in the Year 1380, by John Wiclif D.D.: To which are Prefixed, Memoirs of the Life, Opinions, and Writings of Dr. Wiclif, and an Historical Account of the Saxon and English Versions of the Scriptures, Previous to the Opening of the Fifteenth Century* (United Kingdom: T. Hamilton, 1810), Xlvii.

31   John Wycliffe, "Tracts and Treatises of John de Wycliffe, D.D. with Selections and Translations from his Manuscripts, and Latin Works. Edited for The Wycliffe Society, with an Introductory Memoir, by the Rev. Robert Vaughan, D.D.," Online Library of Liberty, accessed April 5, 2020, https://oll.libertyfund.org/titles/1838 #Wycliffe_0882_499.

and self-indulgent religion espoused by Rome, Wycliffe called his followers to a life of humble faith and self-denial in conformity to the example set by Christ. For him, following Christ was not found in conforming to the traditions of a worldly church structure, but in simple devotion to the person of Christ in His incarnation. He wrote:

> Forsake we ourselves in what we have made ourselves by sin, and dwell we such as we are made by grace. If a proud man be converted to Christ, and is made meek, he hath forsaken himself. If a covetous man ceaseth to covet, and giveth his own things, he hath denied himself. If a lecherous [drunkard] man changeth his life to chastity, he hath denied himself. . . . The cross of Christ is taken when despisings for the love of truth be not forsaken, when the flesh is punished by abstinence, and when compassion and pity toward our neighbour is truly kept; when a man is crucified to the world, and the world is crucified to him, setting at nought the joy thereof. It is not enough to bear the cross of painful life, except men follow Christ in virtues, not by steps of bodily feet, but by meekness, love, and heavenly desire. . . . Heavenly desire raiseth the soul on high, and maketh it to forget the world, and all the likings thereof. He taketh the cross, and is ready to meet all peril for God, and if need is, to die rather than to forsake Christ. And whosoever taketh

not thus his cross, and followeth not Christ thus, is not worthy to be His disciple.[32]

Wycliffe was immovable in his conviction that the exercise of saving faith in Christ would result in a life that is noticeably different than a believer's pre-conversion state. Along with the Apostle Paul in Romans 6, he declared, "The most merciful Lord forgiveth sin to men flying to penitence, but makes us not so sure of the Lord's mercy that we keep sins."[33] This written work helped to clarify what a genuine Christian is and how he or she should live.

FEARLESS GUARDIAN OF TRUTH

In these polemic writings, Wycliffe unsheathed the sword of truth and wielded it as he fought for the faith. In the face of mounting opposition, he proved to be a fearless champion of the saving gospel of Jesus Christ. As he advanced to the frontlines, Wycliffe was willing to risk his favored position and highly-respected status to be a faithful soldier of the Lord. He often stood alone as he found himself surrounded by many foes, both inside and outside the church. But in firmly holding his position, he rallied others to join his ranks, defending the high ground of biblical fidelity—no matter the cost.

---

32 John Wycliffe, quoted in Robert Vaughan, *The Tracts and Treatises of John De Wycliffe* (London: Blackburn and Pardon, 1845), 65.

33 Ibid., 66.

To this day, Wycliffe serves as a timeless example of heroic fortitude in the cause of defending the Scripture. May God raise up in future generations such bold warriors for the truth of Scripture who will fight the good fight of faith, for the glory of God alone.

CHAPTER FIVE

Bible Preacher

Whether we regard Wycliffe's constant activity in the pulpit, or the impression his sermons made, he must be pronounced by far the most notable of English preachers prior to the Reformation.[1]

—PHILIP SCHAFF

In the fourteenth century, the pulpit in England was a dark place. Any semblance of biblical preaching had virtually vanished from the religious scene. It was onto such a world stage that John Wycliffe stepped forward to restore the preaching of the Word of God to its rightful preeminence. Following the work begun by Robert Grosseteste, Wycliffe became "the father of the English pulpit," the first preacher of any note in his native land prior to the Reformation. The many preaching

---

1   Philip Schaff, *History of the Christian Church*, vol. 6, *The Middle Ages* (Peabody, Mass.: Hendrickson, 2006), 328.

luminaries in England who would follow after him—notably Hugh Latimer, George Whitefield, Charles Spurgeon, and Martyn Lloyd-Jones—can trace their preaching heritage back to this dedicated proclaimer of biblical truth.

Wycliffe's sermons were always based upon Scripture, a marked departure from the traditions and practice of that day. Whenever he stood to preach, Wycliffe was relentlessly proclaiming the Bible with unwavering resolve. John Broadus stated that he gave "a new proclamation of the pure gospel" with a dynamic force that was "singularly vigorous."[2] Wycliffe was undeterred in his personal devotion and energy when he stood before an open Bible. Phillip Schaff described Wycliffe's pulpit delivery as "simple and direct," unlike the flowery, soaring oratory of the day. This Bible-commitment gave him a wide appeal and popular acceptance with the common people.[3]

Broadus further depicted Wycliffe's preaching as being "acute in argument," while marked by "bold antagonisms, hard hits, and unsparing sarcasms."[4] He was "the master of argumentation," Broadus added, saying Wycliffe possessed much "popular power and skill" in his delivery.[5] As he expounded

---

2   John Broadus, *Lectures of the History of Preaching* (New York: Sheldon & Company, 1876), 188.

3   Schaff, *History of the Christian Church*, vol. 6, *The Middle Ages*, 328.

4   John Broadus, *Lectures of the History of Preaching* (New York: Sheldon & Company, 1876), 188.

5   Ibid.

the Bible, England had rarely heard this kind of preaching.[6] Wycliffe greatly impacted the British Isle with the legacy of his compelling Bible teaching.

PRESERVATION CHALLENGES

Because Wycliffe's life preceded the arrival of the printing press, the number of his surviving sermons is limited. His sermons were hand-copied by his followers and lacked a system to catalogue them. Over time, it became difficult to determine which sermon manuscripts had been preached by Wycliffe and which ones belonged to his Lollard followers as they furthered his ministry. Copies of his sermons exist in various university libraries throughout Europe with minute differences between them, which testifies to the accuracy with which they had been reproduced and preserved.

Many of Wycliffe's written works, discussed in previous chapters, began as his sermons and were later turned into publications and tracts. In the study of Medieval literature and history, Wycliffe and Lollard texts have become a specialized academic discipline. An additional technical problem is that Wycliffe's sermons were delivered in Middle English, which makes them beyond the readability of the average person today. These challenges make the research of Wycliffe's pages and fragments exceedingly difficult.

---

6   Schaff, *History of the Christian Church*, vol. 6, *The Middle Ages*, 328.

The most recognized record of Wycliffe's preaching is a compilation of 294 sermons compiled by Thomas Arnold in the late nineteenth century.[7] These expositions have preserved a much needed window into Wycliffe's pulpit. These remains of Wycliffe's ministry give evidence of the power of his pulpit as one of history's most influential preachers.

In order to appreciate how revolutionary the impact of Wycliffe was upon the English pulpit, we must first recognize how dismal the religious scene was when he stepped into it.

THE DECLINE OF PREACHING

As Wycliffe surveyed his spiritual context in the fourteenth century, he was deeply concerned for the bleak state of preaching. He grieved over what passed for pulpit ministry in England and saw it for what it was—a tragic departure from God's intended design as found in Scripture. Biographer John Laird Wilson summarized Wycliffe's estimate of the decline of preaching in England at the time: "He lamented the degenerate condition of the pulpit; and he was grieved with the endowed clergy for their habitual neglect of what he considered the principle part of the ministerial work. He denounced all sermons that did not expound the Scripture. He believed they should be rejected."[8]

---

7   Anne Hudson, "A Lollard Sermon-Cycle and Its Implications," *Medium Ævum* 40, no. 2 (1971): 142–56, accessed July 14, 2020, doi:10.2307/43627721.

8   John Laird Wilson, *John Wycliffe, Patriot and Reformer: "The Morningstar of the Reformation"* (New York: Funk & Wagnalls, 1884), 153.

For those who failed to preach the Scripture, Wycliffe minced no words. He scathingly denounced them as "open fools," who "plainly act against Christ's gospel." Further, "If they maintain this error, they are cursed of Him, and are perilous hypocrites and heretics."[9] About this failure by the priests to preach the Bible, Wycliffe cried out: "Men are accounted heretics who act against the pope's law, and it says plainly that each who comes to the priesthood, takes the office of a beadle or crier, to go before doomsday, to proclaim to the people their sins and the vengeance of God. Why then are not the priests heretics who leave the preaching of Christ's gospel, and compel true men to leave preaching the gospel?"[10]

ABANDONING THE TRUTH

The answer to this rhetorical question was clear. In Wycliffe's mind, the priests had become heretics because they had abandoned the preaching of biblical truth. For a man so committed to the Bible, Wycliffe believed there could be no greater indictment against a minister than his failure to preach the Word. He urged preachers to not forsake the preaching of the Scripture, nor to contort its message. Such a departure was a rank dereliction of their pastoral duties, which would surely bring the Lord's severe judgment on the last day.

Because the Word was not being preached, Wycliffe

---

9   Wycliffe, *Of Feigned Contemplative Life*.
10 Ibid.

concluded that this silence was the primary cause of the spiritual drought in the churches of England. Herbert Workman noted, "In Wycliffe's judgment, the lack of preaching based upon the word alone was the cause of spiritual deadness of the age; it was as if one were to prepare a meal without bread. God's word, especially the Gospels, is the seed which brings regeneration and spiritual life."[11] Wycliffe was determined to expel this foul stench of death that hovered over the pulpit. In this desperate hour, only biblical preaching could bring new life to the church, which would, in turn, affect the nation at large.

THE DEBASEMENT OF PREACHING

What these priests and leaders of the day were in pretense, John Wycliffe was in truth. With his personal piety, scholarly mind, and boldness in the pulpit, Wycliffe embodied the characteristics of a Bible-driven preacher. Sadly, few in his day followed his example and, instead, took the opposite path, to the detriment of the church. Rather than addressing the Bible's teaching on sinful matters, Rome was instituting a series of outward moral reforms that they believed addressed the problems at hand. For example, the morality of the priesthood experienced sharp decline as the church began adopting practices that eventually resulted in the required celibacy of the priesthood.

---

11 Herbert B. Workman, *John Wyclif: A Study of the English Medieval Church*, vol. 2 (Oxford, England: Clarendon, 1926), 211.

Carnality in the Priesthood

Wycliffe realized that the power of the pulpit would extend only as far as the piety of the priests. In Wycliffe's estimation, the ministers' failure in preaching the Word was inseparably connected to their sinful living. Wycliffe believed faithful ministry to be an indivisible bond between the preaching of the Word and the minister's pursuit of personal holiness. He was convinced that the two disciplines of preaching and godly living could not be separated. Consequently, he saw the carnality of the priests as intolerable. Wycliffe writes:

> The sin of the common people is great, the sin of the lords, the mighty and the wise, is greater, but the greatest of all is the sin of the prelates [a high-ranking member of the clergy], and most blinding to the people. Therefore are true men by God's commandment bound to cry out the loudest against the sin of the prelates, because it is in itself the greatest, and of greatest mischief to the people.[12]

With clear spiritual vision, Wycliffe saw that the corruption of preaching was fueled by wickedness in the priests. To stress the importance of the personal godliness of preachers, Wycliffe wrote, "Imitate not the priests whom we see after

---

12 John Wycliffe, quoted in Lechler and Lorimer, *John Wycliffe and His English Precursors*, 119.

the sermon sitting in the ale-house, or at the gaming table."[13] How a minister lived in private was foundational to how he preached in public.

Mysticism of the Priests

At the other end of the preaching spectrum was the false piety of the priests who pursued an ascetic life of monasticism.[14] Wycliffe rejected this kind of mysticism, which placed a higher value on esoteric contemplation over the clear, sanctifying power of God's Word. He openly rebuked those who promoted such a false spirituality in a strong polemic titled *Of Feigned Contemplative Life*:

> When true men teach by God's law, understanding, and reason, that each priest ought to do his might, his understanding, and his will, to preach Christ's gospel, the fiend blindeth hypocrites to excuse themselves by feigned contemplative life; and to say that since it is the best, and they may not do both together, they need for the charity [love] of God, to leave the preaching of the gospel, and to live in contemplation![15]

---

13 Douglas C. Wood, *The Evangelical Doctor: John Wycliffe and the Lollards* (Welwyn, Hertfordshire, England: Evangelical, 1984), 87.

14 Gotthard Victor Lechler and Peter Lorimer, *John Wycliffe and His English Precursors* (London: The Religious Tract Society, 1884), 181.

15 Wycliffe, *Of Feigned Contemplative Life*, original MS in the Library of Corpus Christi College, Cambridge, compiled in "Writings of the Reverend and Learned John Wickliff, D.D."

Here, Wycliffe boldly announced that it was the devil—"the fiend"—who was blinding the priests into living a "contemplative life" instead of focusing upon "God's law." Because of this tragic neglect, the ministers of England had devolved into becoming "hypocrites." They merely play-acted in the pulpit while being devoid of true spiritual life.

Hypocrisy of Superficial Pomp

When the lives of spiritual leadership are a vacuous performance, dead ritualism is the inevitable outcome. In the fourteenth century, the priests were building upon the shifting sand of man-contrived traditions. These empty rituals and legalistic rules were imposed on their largely unconverted listeners who desperately needed Christ. Instead, their hearers were burdened with a complex system of religious obligations that had no basis in biblical truth. This heavy yoke was overbearing and therefore crushing to weary, unsaved souls.

Rebuking such Pharisaical practices, Wycliffe spoke, "It would be much better to attend to the defense and exposition of the Scriptures, since many such charters were necessarily such as could not be executed."[16] In his assessment, he concluded that the ministers must start to preach the Bible or the people would remain spiritually downtrodden.

---

16 John Wycliffe, *Tracts and Treatises of John de Wycliffe: With Selections and Translations from His Manuscripts and Latin Works*, ed. Robert Vaughan (United Kingdom: Society, 1845), XLI.

Bankruptcy of Worldly Wisdom

Having deluded themselves with self-importance and dulled the pulpits with mere performances, the priests filled their public ministries with oratorical techniques and theatrics instead of preaching the Bible. Wycliffe's exalted view of the Scripture led him to condemn the priestly practices of story-telling, reciting poems, or spinning fables that were foreign to Scripture.[17] Wycliffe denounced that kind of empty chatter, declaring that all sermons that did not expound the Word of God should be utterly rejected. These were bold words for that time—and words that need to be heard today.

Wycliffe observed that the rhetorical flourishes of the ministers were overshadowing—and even worse, replacing—the actual words of Scripture in sermons. In other words, the style of the delivery was being elevated above the substance of the sermon. Messages were being weighed down by ornamental language that puffed up the preacher and showcased his delivery instead of illuminating God's truth in the Scripture.[18] Rather than simply being a lampstand, the priests saw themselves as being in the spotlight.

Wycliffe believed there was no greater evil committed by ministers than withholding the Word of God from the people. Instead of serving a spiritual feast of strong meat to starving souls, these false shepherds were feeding their congregations a

---

17 Lechler and Lorimer, *John Wycliffe and His English Precursors*, 178.
18 Lechler and Lorimer, *John Wycliffe and His English Precursors*, 180.

poisonous diet of worldly wisdom. They dispensed meaning-less stories and inane poems devoid of any biblical substance. Even when the Scripture was mentioned in the pulpit, it was grossly mishandled and stripped of its true meaning.

THE DISAPPEARANCE OF PREACHING

Preaching historian John Carrick paints an even worse picture of the preaching of the day. He points out that a biblical pulpit was entirely gone: "[T]he preaching of the faith of Christ had practically disappeared, and though the friars were preachers, their preaching was not the declaration of the truths and doctrines of the faith, but general haranguers on whatever took their fancy, and their great aim was to attract the attention and sustain the interest of their hearers by any means. The result was that their preaching often descended into vulgar jesting and buffoonery."[19]

Spreading Spiritual Disease

This forsaking of Scripture in the pulpit and exalting the cleverness of the messenger was directly confronted by Wycliffe. The Evangelical Doctor diagnosed it as the deadly disease that it was and condemned it with his pen and pulpit. Wycliffe was unyielding in his conviction that "an important preoccupation is the need to distinguish between the authority of God and the authority of lesser [preachers], of however venerable a

---

19 J.C. Carrick, *Wycliffe and the Lollards* (New York: Charles Scribner's Sons, 1908), 106.

pedigree."[20] Simply stated, God's truth must be the authority in the pulpit, not the opinions of the preacher. The contrived and carnal ideas of the priests must be completely forsaken.

Wycliffe was convinced that this lack of Bible-saturated preaching had turned the church into a graveyard. Without the life-giving power of Scripture, preachers would continue to proliferate spiritual death and call it "ministry."

Mere Lecturing in the Pulpit

Wycliffe believed that these lifeless sermons had become more like stale lectures for scholars rather than life-giving sermons to feed and nourish everyday people. He observed that pulpits were filled with "endless logical distinctions and divisions."[21] In other words, these messages were merely parsing meaningless words and splitting hairs. Lechler summarized the preaching of the day as "abstract ideas, formal definitions, learned investigations, syllogistic and dialectical argumentation."[22] This lecturing style in the pulpit remained utterly barren of the truth of Scripture.

Anyone can lecture a congregation, Wycliffe reasoned, but a preacher must be so possessed by the Word of God that he wields it as a weapon to topple Satan's kingdom of darkness. It was to this monumental task Wycliffe called ministers.

---

20 Kantik Ghosh, *Power, Prestige, and Authority in Medieval Manuscripts and Texts*, ed. Felicity Riddy (United Kingdom: Boydell & Brewer, 2000), 20.

21 Ibid., 181.

22 Ibid., 186.

Regeneration of Ministers Needed

The spiritual apostasy in the pulpits of England demanded the regeneration of the ministers themselves. Wycliffe understood that lifeless preachers produced lifeless preaching, which, in turn, yielded lifeless congregations. He urged that ministers preach the gospel to their congregants, starting with themselves. The gospel must first work in the heart of the preacher before it can be expected to work in the souls of the people.

Wycliffe addressed the ministers of England when he wrote in his tract *A Short Rule of Life for Priests, Lords, and Laborers*: "At the end of the day, think about how you have offended God . . . and pray for grace that you may dwell and end in His true service, and real love, and according to your skill, to teach others to do the same."[23]

This work by Wycliffe is filled with strong exhortations to ministers to preach the gospel in order to unleash its saving and transforming power. Wycliffe's words demonstrate the evangelistic zeal of this pre-Reformer. Without the gospel, he knew the church had no hope of being anything but a gathering of spiritually dead souls. Without the resounding call of saving grace, it could not make any impact upon the world.

---

23 John Wycliffe, *Tracts and Treatises of John de Wycliffe: With Selections and Translations from His Manuscripts and Latin Works*, ed. Robert Vaughan (United Kingdom: Society, 1845), 47.

THE RECOVERY OF PREACHING

Having witnessed the decline of preaching, Wycliffe set out to correct this glaring deficiency. He boldly called for true biblical preaching, and sought to revitalize the withering pulpit. Wycliffe wrote, "Among all the duties of the pastor . . . holy preaching is most to be praised."[24] Wycliffe understood the critical importance of the pulpit, because he understood the primary place of God's Word in genuine conversion and spiritual growth.

Restoration of the Pulpit Needed

Despite the many hardships facing preachers, Wycliffe insisted, "Priests should preach from housetops, taking no thought for food or drink, but such preaching requires boldness and martyrdom."[25] No matter what sacrifice they must make, pastors must preach the Word. This is their first job.

Wycliffe's definition of preaching drastically departed from the sterile practice of the lectures provided from pulpits. He believed that true preaching must be full of supernatural power if it is to impart spiritual life. He was convinced that only this kind of preaching possesses regenerating power in its bold proclamation of the truth. In *The Pastoral Office*, he wrote that the task of the preacher is "to purge wisely the

---

24 John Wycliffe, "The Pastoral Office," quoted in Matthew Spinka, ed., *Advocates of Reform: From Wyclif to Erasmus* (Louisville, Ky.: Westminster John Knox, 2006), 48.

25 John Wycliffe, Sermon 63/13, 21, quoted in *English Wycliffite Sermons*, vol. 4, eds. Pamela Gordon and Anne Hudson (Oxford, England: Clarendon, 1996), 80.

sheep of disease, that they may not infect themselves and others as well . . . to defend his sheep from ravening wolves."[26] Wycliffe believed that the pulpit should bring the listener into a direct encounter with God that leads to the forsaking of sin and the pursuit of Christ and personal holiness.

Challenge to the Ministers

Wycliffe challenged ministers to live the message they proclaim. Powerful preaching must be backed by pure living.

Not only must the minister live a holy life, but he must challenge his congregation in the same pursuit. In *On the Truth of Holy Scripture*, Wycliffe declared: "I say here that it is necessary to preach all the way to the very ends of the earth. The more strength sin gathers, the more essential it is to preaching."[27] He believed that the preaching of the Word must be strong enough to counter the effects of sin in the world. Sin will grow in its strength if left unchallenged by the pulpit. Thus, ministers must preach the Word throughout the whole earth.

THE PRIORITY OF PREACHING

Wycliffe taught that preaching the Word is the highest calling of ministers in the church. For this pre-Reformer, there was no

---

26 John Wycliffe, "The Pastoral Office," quoted in Matthew Spinka, ed., *Advocates of Reform: From Wyclif to Erasmus* (Louisville, Ky.: Westminster John Knox, 2006), 48.

27 John Wycliffe, *On the Truth of Holy Scripture*, trans. Ian Christopher Levy, in *John Wycliffe on the Truth of Holy Scripture* (Kalamazoo, Mich.: Medieval Institute Publications, 2001), 291–92.

greater work to be done. Wycliffe's position was clear when he said, "Go and preach, it is the sublimest work."[28] By this, he stated that attending to the pulpit was the most excellent work for any minister. He asserted: "The highest service that men may attain to on earth is to preach the word of God. This service falls peculiarly to priests, and therefore God more straightly demands it of them."[29] The highest work, he maintained, was to be the voice of heaven on the earth—to speak on behalf of God to men and women. No other venture can supersede it.

The Essence of the Ministry

Nick Needham affirms this about Wycliffe's commitment to prioritize preaching when he wrote: "For Wycliffe, the essence of the ordained ministry was preaching the word, rather than celebrating the sacraments; it was preaching that made unbelievers into true Christians, and it was preaching above all that built Christians up in the faith by helping them to understand what it meant."[30]

By the exposition of the Word, Wycliffe believed, the church is most supported. When preaching was strongest, he held, the church was strongest. But when the pulpit was weakened, the church was weakest.[31] Commenting on 2 Corinthians 4:2,

28 Douglas C. Wood, *The Evangelical Doctor: John Wycliffe and the Lollards* (Welwyn, Hertfordshire, England: Evangelical, 1984), 87.

29 John Wycliffe, quoted in Religious Tract Society, *Life and Times of John De Wycliffe* (London: Religious Tract Society, 1851), 99.

30 Nicholas R. Needham, *2000 Years of Christ's Power*, vol. 2 (Fearn, Ross-shire, Scotland: Christian Focus, 2017), 418–419.

31 Ibid.

Wycliffe maintains, "This word of the apostle would plainly instruct the faithful to promulgate the word of God among the people."[32] For Wycliffe, the importance of the Word preached must never be supplanted by any other work.

Stressing the Scripture

The priority that Wycliffe placed on preaching the Word is captured in *John Wycliffe and His English Precursors*: "Before everything else, Wycliffe lays stress upon the truth preaching of the word of God is that function which serves, in a degree peculiar to itself, to the edification of the Church; and this is so, because the word of God is a seed (Luke viii,11, 'The seed is the word of God')."[33]

The contrast was sharp between Wycliffe's priority of Bible preaching and that of other areas of emphasis made by Rome, such as the Eucharist. Against the inordinate concentration on the Mass, which largely involved the sole participation of the priest, Wycliffe countered: "It is a far better thing, therefore, that the people receive God's word than that a solitary person receives Christ's body. And this is the proper duty of the higher ranking clergy, since it pertains to the office of evangelization . . . preaching is more effective in blotting out mortal sins than the Eucharist."[34]

Wycliffe stressed that a parishioner's greatest need was

32 Ibid., 52.
33 Lechler and Lorimer, *John Wycliffe and His English Precursors*, 178.
34 Ibid.

to receive the Word, not watch the priests serve the cup. He opposed the notion of the effectual nature of the Eucharist to "blot out sin." He knew that only by faith in the gospel message of Scripture can the stain of sin be removed from the guilty souls of men. In his mind, this demanded the prioritization of biblical preaching.

THE SOBRIETY OF PREACHING

Wycliffe believed that ministers must preach with the fear of God, knowing that the divine scrutiny of the last day awaits them. He was convinced that ministers must be ever mindful that they will stand before God in the final judgment. They will give a stricter account for their preaching to Jesus Christ, who enlisted them to be His heralds. To Jesus Christ they will answer for the message of their preaching. He held that this sobering reminder must grip the heart of every preacher.

The Coming Judgment

Wycliffe warned that the Word-less preaching in the Roman Catholic Church would be exposed when all ministers stand before the Lord in the coming judgment. On that final day, every preacher will give an account for his ministry. Likewise, the people under his care will answer to the Lord for how they lived their lives. In light of this coming hour, they desperately needed to hear the soul-nourishing words of Scripture. In response to this dilemma, Wycliffe said: "Since, therefore,

God has given to both clergy and laity the knowledge of the faith to this end, that they may teach it the more plainly, and work in faithfulness according to it, it is clear that God, in the day of judgment, will require a true account of the uses to which these goods have been applied."[35]

Prompted by the fear of God, Wycliffe exhorted the preachers in his day: "Since we are certain of the day of doom that it shall come to us, and we will not know how soon, and there we shall have judgement of heavenly life, or else of deep hell that evermore shall last, how busy should we be to make us ready for this!"[36] Wycliffe echoed the words of the apostle Paul, that "knowing the fear of the Lord, we persuade men" (2 Cor. 5:11). So must every minister preach, with a sober sense of the looming reality of this last day.

THE PATTERN OF PREACHING

As a result, Wycliffe believed every minister should follow the pattern of Jesus' earthly ministry. He stated, "Jesus Christ left other works and occupied Himself mostly in preaching, and thus did His apostles, and for this, God loved them."[37] Jesus

---

35 Wycliffe, quoted in "Tracts and Treatises of John de Wycliffe, D.D. with Selections and Translations from his Manuscripts, and Latin Works. Edited for The Wycliffe Society, with an Introductory Memoir, by the Rev. Robert Vaughan, D.D.," Online Library of Liberty, accessed March 24, 2020, https://oll.libertyfund.org/titles/1838 #Wycliffe_0882_262.

36 Ibid., 187.

37 Robert Vaughan, *The Life and Opinions of John de Wycliffe: Illustrated Principally from His Unpublished Manuscripts*, vol. II (London: B.J. Holdsworth, 1828), 15.

prioritized preaching in His earthly ministry, and so must ministers in every subsequent generation. By the timeless example of Christ, Wycliffe concluded that proclaiming the Word is the chief calling of ministers.

Preaching like Jesus

Wycliffe believed the minister must preach in like manner as Jesus. The Lord spoke only the words that the Father gave Him to speak. Even so, the preacher must confine himself to preaching the Word of God. He writes, "Let us rather follow the example of our Lord Jesus Christ, who was humble enough to confess, 'My doctrine is not Mine, but the Father's who sent Me. He who speaks of himself seeks his own glory.'"[38] Jesus had nothing to say apart from the word entrusted to Him by the Father, and this is the pattern that every preacher must follow.

Wycliffe was convinced that to preach the Word—and only the Word—was to faithfully follow the example of Christ. Anything else would be a departure from true faithfulness. John Laird Wilson explained: "Wycliffe maintained that the enduring precedent for true preaching was set by Jesus Christ Himself in His earthly ministry. The Lord Jesus prioritized the proclamation of the word and left many other good works undone."[39]

---

38 Lechler and Lorimer, *John Wycliffe and His English Precursors*, 181.

39 John Laird Wilson, *John Wycliffe, Patriot and Reformer: "The Morningstar of the Reformation"* (New York: Funk & Wagnalls, 1884), 153.

Wycliffe reasoned that this example of Christ in prioritizing the preaching of the Word was "enduring," that is, a perpetual standard for every generation. The fourteenth century was to be no different.

Preaching Commanded by Jesus

Wycliffe stressed that preaching the Word is an act of obedience to Jesus Christ, who commands such ministry. He wrote in *The Pastoral Office* that preaching was "the principal ministry which Christ instituted in his church."[40] He stated: "True men say boldly that true preaching is better than praying by monks, yea, though it come of heart and clean devotion; and it edifies more the people; and, therefore, Christ commanded specially His apostles and disciples to preach the gospel, and not to close them in cloisters, nor churches, nor stones to pray thus."[41]

In the Great Commission, Christ commanded His disciples to preach the Word. Anything else would be in defiance and disobedience to Him. He wrote, "Christ bade them . . . go and preach the gospel freely to all manner of men. And woe be to them that forsake this."[42] This command extends

---

40 John Wycliffe, "The Pastoral Office," quoted in Matthew Spinka, ed., *Advocates of Reform: From Wyclif to Erasmus*, 53.

41 John Wycliffe, quoted in John Laird Wilson, *John Wycliffe: Patriot and Reformer*, 153–54.

42 John Wycliffe, quoted in Caleb Cangelosi, "The Mouth of the Morningstar: John Wycliffe's Preaching and the Protestant Reformation," *Eamon Younis*, February 18, 2019, accessed May 22, 2020, http://eamonyounis.blogspot.com/2019/02/the-mouth -of-morningstar-john-wycliffes.html. From Thomas Arnold, *Select English Works of John Wyclif*, vol. I (N.P.: Salzwasser-Verlag, 2020), 361.

down through the centuries to every preacher today. Wycliffe unequivocally stressed, "Christ commanded all His apostles and priests to go into all the world and preach the gospel."[43] He again emphasized, "It is necessary to preach to the very end of the earth."[44] This is to say, the call to ministry is always accompanied by the command to preach wherever Christ sends His messengers.

Wycliffe wrote in *Of the Truth*, "Since the church was obligated to preach the gospel by the Lord's command long before the promulgation of such laws, it still remains the principal duty of the shepherd."[45] Wycliffe insisted that preachers be stirred to evangelize the lost, not in droning lectures, but with the fervent exposition of Scripture.

THE PREREQUISITE FOR PREACHING

Wycliffe understood the inseparable connection between the personal life of the preacher and the power of his preaching. The minister must be a man of God who is marked by both humility and purity. The Bible says that God rejects the proud, but gives grace to the humble. It was this personal holiness that Wycliffe urged those who stood in the pulpits of England to seek.

---

43 Wycliffe, *Of Feigned Contemplative Life*.

44 John Wycliffe, "Wyclif and the English Bible," quoted in *A Companion to John Wyclif: Late Medieval Theologian*, vol. 4, ed. Ian Christopher Levy (Leiden, Netherlands: Brill, 2006), 376.

45 John Wycliffe, *De Veritate*, II:xxiv.

The Humility of the Preacher

Wycliffe understood that if the Word of God is to be rightly preached, the minister must be humble and stripped of pride.[46] Though many were fooled by the pompous spectacle of Rome's liturgy, Wycliffe saw through its thin veneer of vanity. He believed that the pope—whom he bluntly called the Antichrist—was the ringmaster of the whole prideful delusion that was prevalent in pulpits:

> Let him not be ashamed to perform the ministry of the church, since he is, or at least ought to be, the servant of the servants of God. But a prohibition of reading the Holy Scriptures, and the vanity of secular dominion, and a lusting after worldly appearances, would seem to partake too much of a disposition towards the blasphemous advancement of Antichrist, especially while the truths of a scriptural faith are reputed tares, and said to be opposed to Christian truth by certain leaders, who arrogate that we must abide by their decision respecting every article of faith, notwithstanding they themselves are plainly ignorant of the faith of the Scriptures. But by such means there follows a crowding to the court of Rome, to purchase a condemnation of the sacred Scriptures as heretical;

---

46 Ibid.

and thence come dispensations, contrary to the articles of the Christian faith.[47]

Clothed with Meekness

Wycliffe said men ought to preach with "a 'humble and homely proclamation of the gospel,'" stressing a straightforward simplicity of language.[48] With reverence for the Bible, Wycliffe was careful to keep his personal exposition distinct from the actual words of Scripture itself. He desired that his words and explanations would never be confused with the inspired words of Scripture. Wycliffe compared exposition to a housemaid attending to her master, the Scripture, in his tract *Of the Truth of Scripture*: "Exposition however is not sacred Scripture but [as it were] her herald or handmaid. She does not contradict her lady, but by means of special words borrowed from her, peculiar to and derived from her, reveals, discloses and explains her respectfully."[49]

Wycliffe believed that only as the minister is clothed with meekness can his preaching be life-changing. He noted, "The priests learn and teach Holy Scripture for this purpose, that the Church may learn to know the walk of Christ, and may

---

47 John Wycliffe, *Tracts and Treatises of John de Wycliffe: With Selections and Translations from His Manuscripts and Latin Works*, ed. Robert Vaughan (United Kingdom: Society, 1845), LI.

48 Lechler and Lorimer, *John Wycliffe and His English Precursors*, 183–84.

49 John Wycliffe, quoted in Ghosh, *Power, Prestige, and Authority in Medieval Manuscripts and Texts*, ed. Felicity Riddy, 19.

be led to love Christ Himself."[50] Wycliffe noted the primary goal in exposition is greater passion for the person and work of Jesus Christ.

Stirred by the lofty supremacy of Christ in preaching, Wycliffe exhorted his fellow Bible preachers to an abiding humility. He called them to remember that all true preaching from Scripture is merely a conduit through which Christ Himself ministers to His church. He stated, "Therefore, let not the preachers be proud of their voices, since it is Christ who is speaking through them."[51] Like the Apostle Peter writing in 1 Peter 4:11, Wycliffe believed that the faithful preacher is simply a lowly mouthpiece for God.

The Purity of the Preacher

In a time when the academic towers of Oxford glistened with polished and pompous learning, Wycliffe's passion was focused upon the purity of the preacher's life. The heart of the preacher must be pursuing personal holiness if he is to have power in the pulpit. His call to fellow preachers was that they must cleanse their own lives of all internal impurities:

> [T]he first condition of the pastor is to cleanse his own spring [inner person], that it may not infect the word of God. . . . God ordains for a good reason that

---

50 Ibid.

51 John Wycliffe, *On the Truth of Holy Scripture*, trans. Ian Christopher Levy, in *John Wycliffe on the Truth of Holy Scripture* (Kalamazoo, Mich.: Medieval Institute Publications, 2001), 282.

by the teaching of the pastor and his own manner of life his preaching to his sheep may be made efficacious, since this acts more effectively than mere preaching. . . . The life of a good pastor is of necessity a mirror to be imitated by his flock.[52]

Wycliffe reaffirmed his conviction that ministers must pursue godly lives when he wrote, "But in this life, the best life for priests is holy life, in keeping God's commands, and true preaching of the gospel, as Christ did, and charged all his priests to do."[53] Here, Wycliffe stressed that priests must focus upon their own personal holiness before the all-seeing eyes of God. In short, every minister must practice what he preaches.

Modeling the Message

Wycliffe believed that the preacher must model the message he preaches. Unlike his counterparts in the Roman Catholic Church, Wycliffe stressed the importance of the preacher's own personal holiness. He wrote:

A priest should live holy, in prayer, in desires and thought, in godly conversation and honest teaching, having God's commandments and His gospel ever on

---

52 John Wycliffe, "The Pastoral Office," quoted in Matthew Spinka, ed., *Advocates of Reform: From Wyclif to Erasmus*, 48.

53 Wycliffe, *Of Feigned Contemplative Life*.

his lips. And let his deeds be so righteous that no man may be able with cause to find fault with them, and so open his acts that he may be a true book to all sinful and wicked men to serve God. For the example of a good life stirreth men more than true preaching with only the naked word.[54]

An important aspect of the preacher's personal godliness must be his love demonstrated toward those whom he serves. Wycliffe understood that the preacher must speak the truth in love. He wrote, "After your sermon is ended, visit the sick, the aged, the poor, the blind and the lame and succour them."[55] Without love, the preacher is only a noisy gong or a clanging cymbal (1 Cor. 13). His love must be more than mere words, but be demonstrated in action and deeds.

THE CONTENT OF PREACHING

While the priests of the Roman Catholic Church busied themselves with rites and rituals, Wycliffe repeatedly emphasized that the main vocation of the minister was to preach the Word. According to James Henthorn Todd, "Over and against the tradition of the church, Wycliffe promoted the preaching of God's word as the supreme task when he said, 'And also I

---

54 Wycliffe, quoted in Schaff, *History of the Christian Church*, vol. 6, 329.
55 Douglas C. Wood, *The Evangelical Doctor: John Wycliffe and the Lollards* (Welwyn, Hertfordshire, England: Evangelical, 1984), 87.

say, that every deacon and priest is more bound to preach the word of God than to say his canonical hours, according to the primitive order of the church.'"[56]

Wycliffe was committed to *sola Scriptura* in preaching long before the Reformers were committed to this same governing principle. He called his fellow clergy to the same high standard of integrity to Scripture.

Wycliffe was possessed by a high view of biblical preaching because he had such a towering view of Scripture. These two commitments go hand-in-hand together—the latter inevitably producing the former. Though he was knowledgeable in the traditions of the church, Wycliffe nevertheless believed there was no higher authority than inspired Scripture. Everything yielded to biblical truth. Preaching the Word was therefore the most important work of the minister. It was by the written Word that the living God spoke to His church—and this was principally by preaching in a manner understandable to the people.

This was vastly different from the practice of the Roman Catholic Church that had prioritized the place of the Latin Mass in the worship service. Tragically, the hierarchy of Rome saw the altar as a greater means of grace than the verbal proclamation of the Word. Thus, the pulpit was often uprooted and moved to the side of the sanctuary, and the altar was placed in the central place. But with great tenacity, Wycliffe challenged this unbiblical priority. He rebuked the elevated importance

---

56 James Henthorn Todd, "An Apology for Lollard Doctrines, Attributed to Wicliffe: Now First Printed From a Manuscript in the Library of Trinity College, Dublin," Xxxiv.

of the Mass over the pulpit. He called the church to take up the prophetic mantle of preaching the Word that had been given to them by God.

Possessed with Bible Knowledge

Wycliffe was convinced that the duty to preach necessitated that the ministers must possess a thorough knowledge of biblical truth. It would be their depth of knowledge in the Word of God that would largely govern the power of their preaching. Wycliffe wrote:

> Inasmuch as the duty of a shepherd is one which required driving, feeding, and defending his flock, this spiritual duty cannot possibly be fulfilled without a knowledge of Holy Scripture. . . . And since the title of the office is "shepherd," it is clear that God cannot create a shepherd, unless he would then feed his flock. . . . Now it is clear that the spiritual pastures through which one ought to drive the Lord's flock are the truths of Scripture and the way of the Lord, and not the path which leads to hell. By the same rationale, spiritual sustenance is . . . in the preaching of God's word.[57]

There can be no true preaching apart from rightly understanding and properly expounding the written Word of God.

---

57 John Wycliffe, *De Veritate*, II:xxi.

Following a Literal Interpretation

As Hudson points out, Wycliffe's commitment to Scripture continued to resonate through his followers, the Lollards, when they wrote, "'All holy writ is true after [to] the letter.'"[58] It was also their contention that the church of the day was on the verge of destroying God's Word because they did not preach the Word of God as the sufficient, binding authority of all men."[59] Ironically, the Lollards were even commended by many of their opponents for their unwavering commitment to the Word of God.

Wycliffe opens one of his most notable works, *Of the Truth of Sacred Scripture*, by stating: "Scripture is true in all of its parts according to the intended literal sense. This is why professors of Holy Scripture ought to imitate its manner of speaking, adhering to its eloquence and logic, more so than any foreign pagan writing."[60]

So committed was Wycliffe to preaching the Scripture exclusively that Hudson observes the "complete absence of fables . . . no Lollard sermon contains any story material from outside the Bible—no classical anecdote, no pious saint's life story, no moral exemplum. Even when the occasion in question would seem to require it . . . this rule is maintained."[61] From this, they were known to be "Bible men," those saturated with

---

58 Quoted from Bodleian manuscript 288, f. 73ra, Ibid., 271.
59 Ibid., 271.
60 John Wycliffe, *De Veritate*, I:i.
61 Hudson, *The Premature Reformation: Wycliffite Texts and Lollard History*, 269–70.

Scripture. They were men who exemplified what Spurgeon would later describe in John Bunyan: "Prick him anywhere—his blood is Bibline, the very essence of the Bible flows from him."[62]

Committed to Bible Preaching

In keeping with the priority of preaching, Wycliffe believed there must be the practice of true preaching, which is biblical preaching. Wycliffe believed that only the written Word must be preached. He was convinced the Bible is the living seed that alone imparts spiritual life. It is pure milk that nourishes the soul and meat to grow strong faith. Because the chief business of the preacher is to care for souls, it is God's Word they must preach—only then will they succeed in their God-given calling. Wycliffe would say in one of his sermons that, "The authority of Scripture is unquestionable. . . . Scripture contains all truth."[63] He knew that only Scripture contains divine life, and it alone is able to impart new life to spiritually dead souls (1 Pet. 1:23-25).

As noted by Wycliffe scholar Anne Hudson, the substance of Wycliffe's sermons was strictly biblical. She writes: "Wyclif's byname, Doctor Evangelicus, reflected the primacy

---

62 "Mr. Spurgeon as a Literary Man," in *The Autobiography of Charles H. Spurgeon, Compiled from His Letters, Diaries, and Records by His Wife and Private Secretary*, vol. 4, *1878–1892* (Curtis & Jennings, 1900), 268.

63 John Wycliffe, Sermon 92/58, 93/77, 120/16, quoted in *English Wycliffite Sermons*, vol. 4, eds. Pamela Gordon and Anne Hudson (Oxford, England: Clarendon, 1996), 71.

that he had put upon both the gospel message and the open preaching of that message; this lesson, if no other, was never forgotten by his followers—even their enemies testify to their diligence in the matter."[64]

Maintaining Sequential Exposition

For Wycliffe, it was non-negotiable that ministers preach from the Bible sequentially. They must preach in a consecutive manner through a portion of the Scripture. He insisted that ministers preach in a verse-by-verse fashion, giving careful attention to the immediate context of the passage and the building argument of the author and the book. Rather than pulling verses out of their context, the expositor must interpret each passage within the literary unit in which it is found. Likewise, the preacher must consider the larger place the passage finds itself in that particular book in the Bible and within the whole Bible.

Hudson writes that Wycliffe adopted this approach of sequential exposition to preaching. Further, he required it of the Lollard preachers who were trained and commissioned by him. Hudson comments: "The structure of the Lollard sermon is the 'old' style where the basic pattern is of sequential exegesis, and not the 'new' style in which an elaborate schema

---

64 Anne Hudson, *The Premature Reformation: Wycliffite Texts and Lollard History* (Oxford, England: Clarendon, 1988), 269.

of the preacher's own devising with complicated divisions and subdivisions is imposed."[65]

Simply put, Wycliffe believed that the Bible will most naturally speak for itself and yield its God-given message when it is preached in a consecutive manner within its context.

Teaching Sound Doctrine

For Wycliffe, preaching and theology were inseparable entities. He wrote in *Of the Truth*, "First it seems that every priest or curate would have to be a theologian, because he preaches the gospel. . . . To this I say that the assumption is true, because every Christian must be a theologian."[66] He believed there can be no preaching without sound theology, nor fruitful Christian living. Lechler explains, "To bring out the doctrine of the Scriptures (*fides Scriptura*) as of supreme authority, is his highest aim. His sermons are saturated with Bible thoughts and interwoven with Bible reminiscences."[67]

Wycliffe held that every preacher must grow in his knowledge of theology, "Otherwise, given his ignorance of the sense of Scripture, he could be mistaken and thereby deceive people by preaching some perverted meaning."[68] Doctrinal errors must not be tolerated for any minister. Such malpractice

---

65 Ibid., 270–71.
66 John Wycliffe, *De Veritate,* II:xxiv.
67 Lechler and Lorimer, *John Wycliffe and His English Precursors*, 185.
68 Ibid.

would be akin to a doctor prescribing fatal poison rather than good medicine.

THE CLARITY OF PREACHING

Wycliffe stressed that the church is most healthy when the Word is most clearly preached: "The church . . . is honored most by the preaching of God's word, and hence this is the best service that priests may render unto God."[69] By this primary emphasis upon biblical preaching, Wycliffe resolved to reform the church. More than any leader at the time, Wycliffe was mightily used to recover pure, biblical preaching in England.

Language of the Marketplace

Wycliffe was revolutionary in that he believed in the importance of preaching in the language of laymen. During his lifetime, Middle English was the language of the marketplace. For Wycliffe, preaching that was veiled in Latin, a language not understood by the populace, was not preaching at all. In Wycliffe's understanding, true preaching came from explaining Scripture in the language of the people. The delivery of the message must come with clear and coherent meaning to the people—or it has no impact.

Commenting on Wycliffe's fundamental commitment to preach in the native tongue of his countrymen, Lechler noted:

---

69 Robert Vaughan, *The Life and Opinions of John de Wycliffe: Illustrated Principally from His Unpublished Manuscripts*, vol. II, 15.

"In the English sermons, we find still more frequently a plain and popular, even a drastic style of speaking, and a moving, heart-felt tone, especially when the preacher anticipates the judgment seat and the last account."[70] This was a groundbreaking approach to the pulpit and long overdue.

From this point on, all preaching had to be done in the everyday vernacular of the people for whom it was understood. In like manner, Wycliffe believed the Bible itself should be rendered in the readable and discernable language of the common people.

Clear and Distinct Words

As Wycliffe developed his approach to the pulpit, he was committed to preaching that was easily understood by the average person. Carrick says, "Wycliffe's position was a clear, distinct, and firm one, namely, that the plain and simple preaching of the gospel was the best means of reaching the hearts and consciences of men and women."[71] Wycliffe was convinced that the power of salvation resided in the message, not in the messenger. Vacuous oratorical flairs were to be set aside in favor of the easily understood preaching of the Word.

Stephen Lahey writes of Wycliffe, "His style was to avoid referring to church fathers, Franciscan ideals, or other topics not immediate to his exegesis, which earned him the nickname

---

70 Lechler and Lorimer, *John Wycliffe and His English Precursors*, 187.
71 Carrick, *Wycliffe and the Lollards*, 175.

'clear and plain doctor.'"[72] Nicholas of Lyra, a Franciscan known for his rejection of the rhetorical flourishes, described Wycliffe as "a copious and gifted postulator of Scripture."[73] This plain-spoken method in the pulpit would be the hallmark of Wycliffe's preaching ministry. Wycliffe says: "As now the sowing of God's word is the appointed means for the glory of God and the edification of our neighbor, it is plain that the sowing is all the more aptly done the more shortly and completely it fulfills that end. Without doubt, this is the case with a plain and simple mode of address (*plana locutio*); and this mode therefore ought to be chosen."[74]

This legacy of clarity in the pulpit was passed on to Wycliffe's followers, known as the Lollards, as they were dispersed across England and Europe. He instructed them to preach plainly, "By authority of the law of God men should speak her words as God's law speaks, and strange not in speech from the understanding of the people, and always beware that the people understand well, and so use common speech in their own person."[75]

THE BURDEN OF PREACHING

As Wycliffe stood to preach, he was burdened for the eternal destiny of his listeners. With an impending sense of final

---

72 Stephen E. Lahey, *John Wyclif* (New York: Oxford University Press, 2009), 149.

73 Ibid.

74 Lechler and Lorimer, *John Wycliffe and His English Precursors*, 183.

75 John Wycliffe, *Select English Works of John Wyclif*, vol. 1 (Oxford, England: Clarendon, 1869).

judgment he said, "it is essential to teach people that they must turn away from the broad path of sin that leads to hell."[76]

Preaching the Gospel

He expressed his passion in the pulpit as "bringing men cleanly to the Gospel, and the peace and freedom of Christ's order, that being the most perfect, and the most easy to win heaven by."[77] For him, "The proclamation of the gospel is the most important pastoral duty."[78] With a desire to see lost sinners come to faith in Christ, he declared, "Preachers should not preach for worldly goods or to get worldly fame nor to stir men to fight, but [for the sinner] to make peace with God."[79] Wycliffe's supreme desire was for the hearts of his hearers to be reconciled to the Lord.

Preaching God's Grace

Far from Rome's efforts at self-righteousness and its false system of penance and purgatory, Wycliffe pronounced the message of God's free grace in His saving gospel. Stressing God's willingness to show mercy, he said, "He is all-merciful.

---

76 John Wycliffe, *On the Truth of Holy Scripture*, trans. Ian Christopher Levy, in *John Wycliffe on the Truth of Holy Scripture* (Kalamazoo, Mich.: Medieval Institute Publications, 2001), 297.

77 John Wycliffe quoted in *Tracts and Treatises of John de Wycliffe: With Selections and Translations from His Manuscripts, and Latin Works*, ed. Robert Vaughan (United Kingdom: Society, 1845), 8.

78 John Wycliffe, *Iohannis Wyclif Sermones Now Edited from the Manuscripts with Critical and Historical Notes*, vol. I, ed. Iohann Loserth (London: Wyclif Society, 1887), III.

79 John Wycliffe, Sermon E51/80, quoted in *English Wycliffite Sermons,* vol. 4, eds. Pamela Gordon and Anne Hudson (Oxford, England: Clarendon, 1996), 80.

Why? Because He is more ready to receive sinful men to grace, that they would truly leave their sins, than they are to ask for mercy."[80] Wycliffe expounded the life-giving gospel that invites weary sinners to come to the Fountain of living waters, where they may drink freely without cost. Instead, the preaching of his day called men to come to the broken cisterns of man's attempts to save himself (Jer. 2:13).

Wycliffe urged those to whom he preached to call out to God for His grace to pardon sin. He urged: "[C]ry heartily to God for grace and power to leave all sin, and ever after to live in virtue. And after this, be about speaking to bring your neighbours to better living. And if they are at debate, bring them by thy power to love and charity and concord."[81] Wycliffe understood that those living in sin must turn to God in repentance and faith.

Preaching the New Birth

For Wycliffe, the life-giving seed of the Word alone produces the new birth. He wrote in *Of the Truth*, "Therefore, the priest

80 John Wycliffe, "Expositio Decalogi," quoted in John Wycliffe, "Tracts and Treatises of John de Wycliffe, D.D. with Selections and Translations from his Manuscripts, and Latin Works. Edited for The Wycliffe Society, with an Introductory Memoir, by the Rev. Robert Vaughan, D.D.," Online Library of Liberty, accessed May 22, 2020, https://oll.libertyfund.org/titles/wyclife-tracts-and-treatises-of-john-de-wycliffe.

81 John Wycliffe, "Expositio Decalogi," quoted in John Wycliffe, "Tracts and Treatises of John de Wycliffe, D.D. with Selections and Translations from his Manuscripts, and Latin Works. Edited for The Wycliffe Society, with an Introductory Memoir, by the Rev. Robert Vaughan, D.D.," Online Library of Liberty, accessed May 22, 2020, https://oll.libertyfund.org/titles/wyclife-tracts-and-treatises-of-john-de-wycliffe.

should give heed to that task above all others, and not lapse into idleness. On this basis, the minor premise is clear: that is the work which most directly produces children of God."[82] This lofty and noble "work" about which Wycliffe speaks is the minister's "task" of preaching the gospel, which is "above all others" in its importance. Only the Scripture possesses the supernatural life within it to birth spiritual "children of God" into His family.

Again, Wycliffe asserted, "Christ preached the gospel, and charged all his apostles and disciples to go and preach the gospel to all men; then it is the best life for priests in this world, to preach the gospel."[83] The greatest news that could ever come from a minister is the gospel of Jesus Christ. Wycliffe said men should preach "the truth which edifies."[84] This high ground of preaching the gospel must never be forsaken.

Preaching to the Heart

Regarding gospel preaching, Wycliffe believed that it must dive deeper than simply providing cognitive instruction to the mind. The exposition of the gospel must aim at piercing the heart, where the conviction of sin must occur. Wycliffe said, "In every proclamation of the gospel, the true preacher must address himself to the heart, so as to flash the light into the spirit of the hearer, and to bend his will into obedience to the

---

82 John Wycliffe, *De Veritate*, II:xxi.

83 From the tract "Of Feigned Contemplative Life."

84 Ibid., 183.

truth."[85] For Wycliffe, preaching must not lie on the surface of his hearers, but penetrate to the depths of the soul and expose the heart. Only then could there be the conversion of the soul under the preaching of the Word.

THE CONTROVERSY OF PREACHING

The inevitable result of Wycliffe's preaching the gospel of grace and the full counsel of God's Word was controversy. Conflict cannot be avoided when it exposes the false gospel of salvation by man's own works. This clash with false religion is what Wycliffe faced and sought to prepare other preachers to endure. Included in the responsibility of preaching the truth is paying a high price to trumpet its call.

Preaching the Final Judgment

Wycliffe declared that all preachers should boldly warn their hearers of that judgment to come. He said, "They should preach the terror of everlasting punishment . . . this is a special medicine employed as an antidote against the errors of the sheep. It is meant to frighten them with the very opposite of consolation . . . though hardened by their vices, they are led back to Christ by revealing the grievousness and everlasting duration of hell's punishment when compared to a bit of fleeting happiness."[86]

---

85 Wilson, *John Wycliffe: Patriot and Reformer*, 156.
86 Ibid.

Preaching Creates Conflict

Wycliffe believed preachers must sound a clarion note of warning to their listeners, while they are being lulled to sleep in the church. Sinners who are perishing without Christ must be awakened from their slumber. Wycliffe remarked: "It is one thing to sing a spiritual song [a sermon designed to exalt God], and another to speak a word of warning [lest they perish eternally]. The measure of verse has, it is true, a certain charm, but only a sensuous charm, which rather draws off the soul of the hearer from the spiritual and the eternal subject of discourse, and destroys his taste for spiritual nourishment."[87]

Here, Wycliffe emphasized the importance of preaching not only to promote the worship of God, but to issue the sober warnings of Scripture. One must not be preached at the expense of the other. Both aspects are necessary to produce genuine converts and mature believers. But such preaching is certain to create conflict with the religious establishment. Wycliffe repeatedly made clear that such conflict was not an inherent flaw in the truth preached, but in the hearer who received it. He wrote: "it seems fair to say that if anything true sounds wrong, the reason for this rests with the person who is listening to it. For God approves every truth . . . if indeed anything true sounds wrong to a person on his part, this is because the truth within him has been damaged."[88]

---

87 Ibid., 182.

88 John Wycliffe, *On the Truth of Holy Scripture*, trans. Ian Christopher Levy, in *John Wycliffe on the Truth of Holy Scripture* (Kalamazoo, Mich.: Medieval Institute Publications, 2001), 177.

Surrounded by the apostate Roman Catholic Church that had forsaken the true gospel, Wycliffe undertook the cause of preaching the purity of the saving grace of God. He asserted in a sermon that, "Antichrist [the pope] desires to substitute his contrary law for Christ's [word]. This hinders the keeping of Christ's [word] and puts men from the freedom of Christ."[89] This kind of explosively provocative preaching toward "Antichrist" produced a certain clash with false religion.

Preaching Exposes Error

Wycliffe understood that if he was called to preach the truth, he must likewise expose the damning lies that were being spread from pulpits. In his own preaching, he repeatedly warned fellow believers of the destructive dangers of the heresies in his day. The false teachings of Rome had corrupted the purity of the gospel, and these errors must be confronted. Though he realized such preaching would generate conflict, he wrote, "many more evils arise from not speaking the truth than from its promulgation. It is clear, therefore, that every evil proceeds from not speaking the truth."[90]

Wycliffe disputed the false gospel that was being taught by religious leaders in positions of high authority in the church. "Wycliffe . . . availed himself of preaching as a means of

---

89 John Wycliffe, Sermon E43/81, quoted in *English Wycliffite Sermons*, vol. 4, eds. Pamela Gordon and Anne Hudson (Oxford, England: Clarendon, 1996), 77.

90 John Wycliffe, *On the Truth of Holy Scripture*, trans. Ian Christopher Levy, in *John Wycliffe on the Truth of Holy Scripture* (Kalamazoo, Mich.: Medieval Institute Publications, 2001), 184.

battling with the evils which he saw in the religious condition of the National Church."[91] He understood that the best way to unmask such errors was by teaching sound doctrine. In so doing, he refuted those false shepherds who contradicted the gospel. This defense of the truth stressed the need for careful study of the Scriptures in order to confront the harmful heresies that damn the souls of men.

A New Day for Preaching

A God-inspired Bible demands faithful preaching. Wycliffe rightly understood that the power of God to save did not reside in the messenger, but in the message. He knew that God placed the power to regenerate and sanctify not in His worker, but in His Word. The infallible truth must be preached by fallible men, so the glory will be directed to God alone.

Let us give thanks for the timeless example and enduring legacy of this Morning Star of the Reformation.

---

91 Lechler and Lorimer. *John Wycliffe and His English Precursors*, 176.

CHAPTER SIX

Bible Translator

Let us ever gratefully remember that Wycliffe was the first Englishman who translated the Bible into the English language.[1]

—J.C. RYLE

A man of immense abilities, John Wycliffe fulfilled many strategic roles in his tireless labors for the kingdom of God. He was a professor in the classroom, an author of treatises, and a reformer of the church. Additionally, he was a pastor of a local flock, a preacher in the pulpit, and a statesman for the nation. Each of these duties were vitally important to the advancement of God's work. But the greatest task Wycliffe fulfilled was that of a Bible translator. History records that his most significant contribution was initiating the groundbreaking project of translating the Bible into the English language.

---

[1] J.C. Ryle, *Light from Old Times* (Edinburgh, Scotland: Banner of Truth, 2015), 26.

The need for the truth of the Bible was absolutely essential for the salvation of the English people. If they did not have the Scripture in their own tongue, they would continue to perish in spiritual ignorance. Without access to the Word of God, their souls would be eternally lost. The work of Bible translation into the English language, Wycliffe believed, was an absolutely necessary means of grace for the salvation of his fellow countrymen. Wycliffe wrote, "Spiritual profit is infinitely better than temporal, and spiritual profit cannot be acquired apart from the teaching of Holy Scripture."[2] Without the message of the Bible, the English population could not be saved.

This translation project into the English language was an enormous endeavor involving many people, but the work began under the initiative of Wycliffe. He wrote, "I wish manuscripts of the New Testament or the Old Testament to be read and studied in the common tongue."[3] Having involved himself in the political realm, he proclaimed in one sermon that it was particularly important that, "Lords should know God's law in their mother tongue—then they would perceive the error of those who hide Scripture from seculars."[4] Until the time of his death, Wycliffe provided the primary impetus

---

2   Wycliffe, cited in "Wyclif and the English Bible," in *A Companion to John Wyclif: Late Medieval Theologian*, vol. 4, ed. Ian Christopher Levy (Leiden Netherlands: Brill, 2006), 376.

3   Ibid., 377.

4   John Wycliffe, Sermon 45/36, quoted in *English Wycliffite Sermons*, vol. 4, eds. Pamela Gordon and Anne Hudson (Oxford, England: Clarendon, 1996), 78.

and inspiration for this monumental undertaking. However, it was a labor so great that it required the participation of many proficient scholars. This work was so demanding that it would necessitate ongoing labor after his death.

THE MOTIVATING REASON

This translation work grew out of Wycliffe's strong desire that his countrymen—regardless of their social class or occupation—would know Jesus Christ by believing His gospel. For this reason, he devoted himself to this colossal undertaking, which required working from the Latin Vulgate. Wycliffe desired to spread the saving knowledge of the truth all across England. The apostle Paul writes, "Faith comes from hearing, and hearing by the word of Christ" (Rom. 10:17). Wycliffe knew that only by hearing—or reading—the Word of God can anyone exercise saving faith in Him. Therefore, it was necessary to translate the saving words of Scripture into the understandable language of this time in England.

D'Aubigne pinpointed Wycliffe's fervor for the Word, saying, "Above all he loved the Bible, he understood it, and desired to communicate this treasure to others."[5] Wycliffe wanted to offer the spiritual wealth of the gospel to all English-speaking people, from the richest aristocrat to the most impoverished

---

5   J.H. Merle d'Aubigne and S.M. Houghton, *The Reformation in England*, vol. 1 (Edinburgh, Scotland: Banner of Truth Trust, 2015), 74.

farmer. His translation endeavor would be necessary to fulfill this evangelistic mission.

THE MANY CHALLENGES

For hundreds of years previous, the Bible had been regarded as a book exclusively for the clergy. The proper interpretation of its meaning was assumed to be largely dependent on the pope and his elite hierarchy of church leaders.

Forbidding an English Bible (1229)

In 1229, the Council of Toulouse forbade the use of the Bible by laymen, claiming that the laity could not make sense of it. Wycliffe stood in direct opposition to this as an outspoken advocate of an open Bible. He believed that the Word of God is a book to be read, studied, and understood by all Christians. He stressed that as Jesus Christ is offered to all, so should Scripture be offered to all. To withhold the Bible from the laity, Wycliffe taught, is a grave sin.

Widespread Ignorance of Latin

However, an even greater hindrance was the fact that the average person did not know Latin, the language in which the Vulgate was written. In this sense, the Bible was a closed book, inaccessible to the vast majority of people of England. As a result, Wycliffe embarked on the daring journey of rendering the Scripture into the commonly understood language.

The translation work was not without great difficulty. A primary challenge was the fact that copies of the Latin Vulgate were few and far between. Moreover, Erasmus of Rotterdam had not yet gathered together Greek manuscripts from around Europe in order to compile them into a Greek New Testament. These copies would not be available until 1516, a century and a half later. An additional obstacle was that Johannes Gutenberg had not yet invented the printing press with movable type. That would not take place until around the year 1440, over fifty years after Wycliffe's death. As a result, there were very few hand-copied volumes of the Vulgate available in this day from which to work.

Reading a Dead Language

The Latin Vulgate had been translated from copies of the original Greek and Hebrew texts in the fourth century. But because the majority of those in England did not know Latin, it was beyond the comprehension of most people. One historian notes that even the average priest could not easily read Latin, sometimes unable to translate it at all.[6] It was this lack of biblical literacy that challenged Wycliffe to begin his translation mission.

Given this state of spiritual starvation, Wycliffe's heart was heavily burdened to bring people into the saving knowledge of Jesus Christ. Yet without an English Bible, there was no means to this end. Herbert B. Workman notes, "It is impossible to quote any instance of lay people who were acquainted with

---

6   Margaret Deanesly, cited in Herbert B. Workman, *John Wyclif: A Study of the English Medieval Church*, vol. 2 (Oxford, England: Clarendon, 1926), 153–54.

the Bible before Wycliffe's day."[7] This ignorance of the Scripture caused a thick darkness to shroud the land of England.

A readable Bible in the English vernacular for common people and priests alike was an utter necessity for the advance of Christianity. The eternal destiny of souls and the fortitude of the church was at stake. With the nation groping in spiritual darkness, Wycliffe was determined to shine the light of Scripture into every corner of England. Workman writes: "All the evidence shows that Wycliffe's plea for the reading of the Bible by the laity was a revolution, not an extension of an existing practice. When Wycliffe, urged by the logic of his theological positions, determined on this revolution, he was irresistibly driven into translation."[8]

THE LATIN VULGATE

As previously mentioned, the Bible used at this time in England was the Latin Vulgate. The Vulgate had been first compiled by the church father Jerome in the fourth century, with the help of other scholars. Jerome had been commissioned by Pope Damasus I in 382 to revise the old Latin version (*Vetus Latina*) of the four Gospels from the best Greek texts and the Psalms. Other scholars completed the New Testament, while Jerome did much of the revision work of the Old Testament from the Hebrew Bible.

---

7   Ibid., 154–55.
8   Herbert Workman, *John Wyclif: A Study of the Medieval Church*, vol. II (Eugene, Ore.: Wipf & Stock, 1926), book III, 155.

Scarcity of Latin Copies

This version of the Bible became known as the Latin Vulgate—"Vulgate" meaning common or colloquial speech—and was used by the Roman Catholic Church in Wycliffe's day. It was from this starting point that Wycliffe began the immense project of translating the Bible into the English language. John Carrick illustrates the scarcity of Bible resources in Wycliffe's day:

> The only Bibles in existence were the hand-written scrolls of the Latin Vulgate, a copy of which was a fortune in itself, a large flock of sheep being oftentimes given in exchange for a single page: to transcribe copies of the Vulgate was considered a work of the greatest merit, and sure to secure an entrance into glory. Of course, these Latin Bibles were quite out of the reach of the people, and were to be found only in the possession of the parish priest, who alone could understand the language.[9]

The Language of the Elite

Latin was the language of the academic classroom. Only members of royal or upper class families understood Latin, because they had privileged access to private tutors and higher education at the universities of Oxford and Cambridge. Moreover, only some members of the clergy understood the Latin Vulgate. Many of them, if not most, could not translate it for

9   J.C. Carrick, *Wycliffe and the Lollards* (New York: Charles Scribner's Sons, 1908), 142.

themselves. If the average farmer, blacksmith, or maiden were to understand the Bible, Wycliffe concluded they must have it in their native tongue. The English people must be able to read for themselves what the Bible says. No longer must they be dependent upon the clergy, who twisted its meaning and corrupted its message. The time for this immense change was now.

Carrick emphasized the importance and unique nature of Wycliffe's work as the seminal beginning of the history of the English Bible: "There were, it is true, small portions of the New Testament in English: even so early as the sixth century the Venerable Bede rendered the Gospel of St. John into Anglo-Saxon; but Wycliffe was the first to give the English people the complete copy of the Holy Scriptures in the native tongue, and to let the common people read with their own eyes the priceless words of everlasting life."[10]

THE WORK BEGUN (1380)

As the initiator of this project, Wycliffe served as its driving force. There is uncertainty regarding the exact part Wycliffe himself played in the page-by-page translation work. Some historians believe that he played a significant role. Others believe he was only the organizer. Nevertheless, this prominent professor was the trailblazing visionary who birthed this translation project for the English people. Possessing a brilliant intellect, he most likely played some part in the technical translation groundwork.

---

10 Ibid.

However, British scholar F.F. Bruce believes that Wycliffe played a minimal role in the translation work. He writes, "It is doubtful if Wycliffe himself took any direct part in the work of Bible translation, but we have no qualms about referring to the Wycliffe Bible, for it was under his inspiration and by his friends and colleagues that the work was done."[11] Scholars are divided on this opinion—many believe he directly translated the biblical text and others conclude he did not.

The Translation Team

To carry out this immense project, Wycliffe recruited a team of scholars from his followers to translate the Latin Vulgate into English. This initial phase of the work took place from 1380 to 1384.[12] Writing of Wycliffe's band of well-educated men, Margaret Deanesly says, "The translators were among the most learned scholars of the day, and their aim was simply to popularize the connected story of the 'meek and poor and charitable living of Christ' and His apostles. They could obtain the picture of this state by a literal and faithful translation, and no temptation to tamper with the text."[13] Wycliffe's aim was not for a loose transliteration of Scripture, but for a precise, even wooden translation. He wanted to preserve the integrity of the text in his translation, while upholding Scripture in the highest esteem.

---

11 F.F. Bruce, *History of the English Bible* (Cambridge, England: Lutterworth, 2002), 13.

12 Workman, *John Wyclif: A Study of the Medieval Church*, vol. II, book III, 156.

13 Margaret Deanesly, *The Lollard Bible: And Other Medieval Biblical Versions* (Eugene, Ore.: Wipf & Stock, 2002), 230–31.

Wycliffe and his team of scholars approached the biblical text with reverential awe. As Workman notes, "Wycliffe's conception of the Scriptures as the final authority led him and his assistants to treat the translation with the utmost reverence."[14] Like Moses stepping onto holy ground at the burning bush, removing his sandals with fear, Wycliffe approached the sacred text, translating it with awe and solemnity.

Nicholas of Hereford

The first of the translation efforts was the work of a coalition, with Nicholas of Hereford (d. 1420) taking the lead in translating much of the Old Testament. He was a brilliant theological scholar who served as a Fellow of The Queen's College at Oxford. Nicholas earned a Doctor of Theology at Oxford in 1382 and was named Chancellor of the University of Oxford that same year. He was an avid reformer of the church, a strong supporter of Wycliffe, and perfectly suited for his part in this groundbreaking venture.

Nicholas's work would come to a swift and dramatic end after he preached a fiery sermon at Oxford in 1382. In the controversial exposition, he criticized the worldliness and extravagant luxury exhibited by the leadership of the Roman Catholic Church. After this explosive diatribe, Nicholas was immediately arrested and appeared at the court of the

---

14 Herbert B. Workman, *John Wyclif: A Study of the English Medieval Church*, vol. 2 (Oxford, England: Clarendon, 1926), 185.

Archbishop of Canterbury. When he refused to repent of his sermon, he was condemned and excommunicated from the church. Nicholas traveled to Rome to appeal his case before Pope Urban, but was rejected and imprisoned for the next five years. After a daring escape from prison in 1385, Hereford returned to England.[15] He was one of the many courageous men surrounding Wycliffe who paid a great price for his commitment to this work.

Other men from Oxford, brilliant in their own right, translated the rest of the Old Testament, as well as the New Testament. We do not know exactly who these men were, but we know the English-speaking world is forever indebted to them for their diligent work.

THE FIRST VERSION (1382)

The first version of Wycliffe's Bible was produced during his lifetime, completed about 1382. D'Aubigne remarked, "The time appeared ripe for the publication of a Bible. The increase of population, the attention the English were beginning to devote to their own language, the development which the system of representative government had received, the awakening of the human mind—all these circumstances favoured the reformer's design."[16]

---

15 Phillip Schaff, "Nicholas Hereford," *The New Schaff-Herzog Encyclopedia of Religious Knowledge*, vol. 8 (Grand Rapids, Mich.: Baker, 1953), 165.

16 D'Aubigné and Houghton, *The Reformation in England*, 1:73.

An Extremely Literal Work

John Carrick recorded, "The New Testament was the work of Wycliffe alone: the Old Testament was translated by his friend Nicholas Hereford and his Lutterworth curate, John Purvey."[17] Purvey described the translating work with Wycliffe as sitting at the opposite ends of the same table with his mentor. He said that each man worked on their respective passages with a bottle of ink in the middle between the two. Despite Wycliffe's handicapped arm, a result of the stroke he suffered, he still wrote diligently.[18] He remained dedicated to his dream of the English Bible, so that he would not allow even this severe physical obstacle to impede him.

The first version of the Wycliffe Bible was "an extremely literal rendering of the Latin original."[19] Great effort was expended to translate the Bible in a manner that preserved the biblical word order and sentence construction. Preserving the verbal accuracy in this new Bible translation was critically important to Wycliffe and his fellow workers. Wycliffe focused on producing a literal rendering of the Latin Vulgate because he took the Word of God so seriously.

Wycliffe's legacy is memorialized in the words of Carrick: "The one great masterpiece of his life will remain and perpetuate his memory as long as time shall last. That work is

17 Carrick, *Wycliffe and the Lollards*, 143.
18 Thom Satterlee, "Purvey Describes His Work with Wyclif," *The Southern Review* 42 no. 2 (Spring 2006): 422.
19 F.F. Bruce, *History of the English Bible*, 15.

his translation of the Bible into English, the first translation of the Scripture into the people's tongue that had ever been made in this land."[20] No greater gift could be given to the English-speaking people than this treasure of truth.

Copied by Hand

Compounding the already mentioned hindrances was the fact that Wycliffe's Bible had to be copied by hand. This by-hand transmission was a painstakingly laborious process that took a considerable amount of time and required a great number of expenses. Carrick recalls the precious few copies that were hand-copied:

> We can hardly estimate the difficulties of such an undertaking as this: there was the heavy opposition of the Church to the popularizing and vulgarizing of the priests' sacred book: there was the entire absence of printer's press and printer's ink, and the like, only the human hand and the slowly moving pen: these and a hundred other difficulties the brave spirit of John Wycliffe faced and overcame; and thus he was the forerunner of all the later translators—the great progenitor of the English Bible of today, the great treasure of the British people.[21]

20   Carrick, *Wycliffe and the Lollards,* 142.

21   Ibid., 143.

Carrick adds this additional insight:

> To multiply copies, Wycliffe got his Oxford students
> and friends to cooperate with him, and thus in time
> they were scattered through the whole land, to so
> great an extent, indeed, that in 1850, when a census
> was taken of the number of written copies in exis-
> tence, no less than a hundred and fifty [manuscripts]
> were found to have survived the wreck of centuries.[22]

D'Aubigne described this laborious process of producing
a Wycliffe Bible:

> As soon as the translation was finished, the labour of the
> copyists began, and the Bible was erelong widely circu-
> lated either wholly or in portions. The reception of the
> work surpassed all expectations. The holy Scriptures
> exercised a reviving influence over men's hearts; minds
> were enlightened; souls were converted; the voices of
> the "poor priests" had done little into comparison with
> this voice; something new had entered into the world.[23]

THE STRONG RESISTANCE

The distribution of the Wycliffe Bible did not go unnoticed
by the dominant religious establishment of the day. This

---

22 Ibid.
23 D'Aubigné and Houghton, *The Reformation in England*, 1:74.

translating endeavor was met with the most aggressive resistance possible. Wycliffe noted the following opposition to a vernacular Bible: "Today it is considered very shocking that the gospel is translated into English and preached to people. . . . Those who preach the gospel in the form and language in which they are better understood are brought low; for friars, bishops and their abettors are shocked that the gospel should become known in English."[24]

Faced with Great Opposition

Augustinian chronicler Henry Knighton, who died shortly after Wycliffe, recorded an early history of the church in England. He documented the great opposition that Wycliffe faced in the spread of his newly translated English Bible. Knighton wrote:

> This master John Wycliffe translated from Latin into English—the Angle not the angel speech—the Scriptures, which Christ gave to the clergy and doctors of the Church that they might sweetly minister to the laity and to the weaker persons according to the message of the season, the wants of men, and the hunger of their souls. Thence by his means it is become vulgar and more open to laymen and women who can read than it is wont to be lettered clerks of good intelligence. Thus the pearl of the gospel is scattered abroad

---

24 Wycliffe, quoted in Margaret Deanesly, *The Lollard Bible: And Other Medieval Biblical Versions* (Eugene, Ore.: Wipf & Stock, 2002), 248.

and trodden underfoot by swine, the jewel of clerics is turned to the sport of the laity, so that what before had been heavenly talent for clerks and doctors of the Church is now the commune aeternum of the laity.[25]

Knighton did not care for Wycliffe and his efforts at church reform. Nevertheless, he respected Wycliffe as an academic scholar and recognized him as an instrumental figure in the national and ecclesiastical life of England. This historian, a contemporary of Wycliffe, wrote that those voicing complaints against the Roman Catholic Church and supporting the principles of Wycliffe numbered practically every other man in England.

THE SECOND VERSION (1388, 1395)

After Wycliffe died in 1384, his secretary John Purvey (c. 1354–c. 1414) led the initial revision of Wycliffe's first edition English Bible and produced two subsequent works in 1388 and 1395. Purvey was a great scholar in his own right, a respected theologian and church reformer who had been Wycliffe's personal assistant. Because of this close proximity to Wycliffe, he was familiar with the entire translation project from its beginning. Purvey was the perfect man to carry on the translation work of Wycliffe and bring it to the next level of excellence.

---

25 Henry Knighton, quoted in Herbert Workman, *John Wyclif: A Study of the Medieval Church*, vol. II (Eugene, Ore.: Wipf & Stock, 1926), book III, 186.

Revised under John Purvey (1388)

With Wycliffe's earlier support, Purvey began the revision of the first edition in Lutterworth, England, where Wycliffe had pastored. As the first edition was a stiff, literal translation, Purvey refined the revision to be a freer, more natural translation that was more easily readable by the populace. This made the second version more readily accessible to the average reader. Like Wycliffe had been, Purvey was also surrounded by a team of Oxford scholars who assisted in these efforts. Purvey secluded himself and began an extensive first revision of Wycliffe's original work, the first of which was completed in 1388, followed by a second revision in 1396.

Purvey wrote that he did this revision work with "much travail," with the aid of "diverse fellows and helpers."[26] He said that he consulted "many old Bibles and other doctors and common glosses."[27] Purvey studied the Latin Vulgate in depth, while consulting "old grammarians and old divines" to ascertain "hard words and hard sentences."[28] Only after such diligent study could the text be best understood and be translated into English. Purvey exercised extreme care in carrying out this work.

General Prologue (1395)

In his second revision, Purvey followed principles that he set forth in his General Prologue. In this opening, he defended

---

26 Bruce, *The English Bible*, 17.

27 Ibid.

28 Ibid.

the right of Christians to have God's Word in their native language. Purvey argued that the people must have the Scripture in their own language in order to "save all men in our realm, which God would have saved."[29] The means was by the work of "a simple creature [who] has translated the Bible out of Latin into English."[30] This "simple creature" was Purvey's description of himself, being entrusted with this glorious mission passed down from Wycliffe.

Increasing Resistance (1401)

This second Bible revision was met with continued opposition from the established powers of the day. Parliament, under the influence of King Henry IV (1399–1413), passed a new law in 1401 that made the burning of heretics legal in England. This law was known as *de heretic comburendo* or "The Burning of Heretics" and was aimed at those who distributed or possessed a Wycliffe Bible. Because of the perceived threat of an English Bible, even owning such a book was considered a capital crime punishable by being burned to death.

Forbidding Any English Translation (1408)

In 1408, Thomas Arundell, the archbishop of Canterbury, wrote "The Constitutions of Oxford," which forbade any translation of the Bible into the English language unless

---

29 Margaret Deanesly, *The Lollard Bible: And Other Medieval Biblical Versions* (Eugene, Ore.: Wipf and Stock, 2002), 258.

30 Ibid.

authorized by the bishops: "It is a dangerous thing . . . to translate the text of the Holy Scripture out of one tongue into another, for in the translation the same sense is not always easily kept. . . . We therefore decree and ordain that no man hereafter by his own authority translate any text of the Scripture into English or any other tongue. . . . No man can read any such book . . . in part or in whole."[31]

The church leaders of Purvey's day were desperate to keep their hold of spiritual power over the laity. Even teaching the Bible in English was considered a crime worthy of death.

Lasting Effect Until Tyndale (1526)

Until the sixteenth century, the Wycliffe Bible was the only English Bible that a select few would possess. This changed with the appearance of a new translation by William Tyndale, the first to be rendered from the Greek New Testament (1526). In 1528, Sir Thomas More, Lord Chancellor of England, published *A Dialogue Concerning Heresies* in which he unloaded a vicious attack upon Tyndale for his English version of the New Testament. In this character assassination, More slandered Tyndale, comparing him to the "great arch-heretic Wycliffe," who was driven with "a malicious purpose to translate the Bible into English."[32] In this vicious attack, the name of Wycliffe continued to be assaulted by the leaders of England.

---

31 Quoted in John Fox, *Fox's Book of Martyrs: The Acts and Monuments of the Church* (London: George Virtue, 1844), 727.

32 Quoted in Bruce, *The English Bible*, 22.

However, the spiritual impact of Wycliffe's Bible had a rich ripple effect throughout the English-speaking world. The effect of Wycliffe's work was expansive and enduring. English stalwart J.C. Ryle paid powerful homage to his work when he wrote,

> The true Christian was intended by Christ to prove all things by the word of God, all churches, all ministers, all teaching, all preaching, all doctrines, all sermons, all writings, all opinions, all practices. These are the marching orders. Prove by all by the word of God; measure all by the measure of the Bible; compare all with the standard of the Bible; weigh all in the balances of the Bible; examine all by the light of the Bible; test all in the crucible of the Bible. That which can abide the fire of the Bible, receive, hold, believe, and obey. That which cannot abide the fire of the Bible, reject, refuse, repudiate, and cast way. This is the standard which Wycliffe raised in England. This is the flag which he nailed to the mast. May it never be lowered![33]

This is the challenge every generation of believers faces. Let us grab the hammer, and nail to the mast our conviction that the Bible is the inspired Word of the living God.

---

33 Ryle, *Light from Old Times*, 3–4.

CHAPTER SEVEN

Bible Legacy

*The Lollard preachers went about England in couples,
clad in russet gowns, preaching at fairs, in market-places
and churches and houses, teaching the simple truths of
primitive Christianity with zeal and simplicity.*[1]

—J.C. CARRICK

After the death of John Wycliffe in 1384, the growing movement of Lollard preachers that had begun under his strong convictions continued to move forward through his many followers. These itinerant preachers advanced the work that Wycliffe began by proclaiming the gospel of Jesus Christ throughout England. Though he was no longer alive to spearhead the movement, Wycliffe's Bible-grounded mission remained intact and the message as bold as when he first

---

1   J.C. Carrick, *Wycliffe & The Lollards* (Edinburgh, Scotland: T&T Clark, 1908), 199.

proclaimed it. This marching army of Bible preachers testified to the genuine power of what God began under Wycliffe.

Wycliffe scholar Rudolph Buddensieg painted a vivid portrait of the pre-Reformer and his Lollards when he wrote: "Prelates, priests, and abbots scorned and hated them, but the people loved them and flocked around them. . . . Among the common people their success was enormous, until their adherents were believed to number at least half the population. . . . Their weapon was the Bible in the vernacular."[2] These soldiers of Christ unsheathed the sharp sword of Scripture as they journeyed from town to town, preaching the gospel from the newly-translated Wycliffe Bible. This sharp, two-edged instrument pierced hearers to their very souls and brought many to a saving knowledge of Christ.

In this last chapter, we want to trace the long-term influence of Wycliffe, which would extend to the Reformation in the sixteenth century. From Wycliffe to the Lollards, to Hus, to the Reformers, the legacy of Wycliffe continued to pay long-term dividends that would eventually reach into Europe and far beyond. Like a long-flowing river, the teaching of Wycliffe continued to swell until its current of truth emptied into the Protestant movement. Let us now trace the flow of biblical truth from Wycliffe to the Reformers.

---

2   Rudolph Buddensieg, "Lollards," *The New Schaff-Herzog Encyclopedia of Religious Knowledge*, vol. VII (London: Funk & Wagnalls, 1931), 15.

The Birth of the Movement

The Lollard movement traces its beginning back to Wycliffe's tenure as an Oxford professor, when he first launched his polemic attack against the false teaching of the Roman Catholic Church. Wycliffe's strong convictions were imparted to his students and other professors, which drew many capable men under the influence of his teaching. Carrick writes about the Lollards, "These were chiefly Oxford graduates trained by Wycliffe himself, and sent by him all over the land to preach a plain and simple Christian faith."[3] They embraced his fundamental belief in the supreme authority of Scripture and followed his example in proclaiming it. These faithful men were equipped by Wycliffe in the core tenets of the gospel, and they preached it fearlessly.

A Far-Reaching Movement

Concerning the early beginnings of the Lollard movement, Carrick notes, "Their influence stretched all over England and even to the lowlands of Scotland; and their simple preaching was eagerly listened to by the people, to whom the preaching of a simple gospel was a novelty."[4] This grassroots movement was initially led by Oxford scholars, but it soon spread to the general populace with others joining their cause.

Reformation historian Diarmaid MacCulloch credits the

---

3   J.C. Carrick, *Wycliffe and the Lollards* (New York: Charles Scribner's Sons, 1908), 132.
4   Ibid.

toppling of the papacy's stronghold on European Christianity partly to the Lollard movement and their adherence to *sola Scriptura*. This was a bold stance they assumed long before it was later codified by the sixteenth-century Protestant Reformation. MacCulloch writes that the Lollards were "fired by Wycliffe's insistence that all the Church's teaching and institutions should be tested rigorously against the record of God's purposes in Scripture."[5] This cornerstone doctrine was laid by Wycliffe, its foundation developed by the Lollards, and its truths built into a fortress of strength by the Reformers.

After Wycliffe's death, the Lollards continued Wycliffe's dissent against the church in Rome. They trumpeted his rejection of the Catholic beliefs of transubstantiation, pilgrimages, confessions to priests, and image-worship. Further, these men of strong convictions stood with Wycliffe in comparing the papal hierarchy to the Antichrist. They held firmly to the sufficiency and finality of the saving work of Jesus Christ. They denied the need for priests in the mass or elaborate religious ceremonies not found in Scripture. In short, the Lollards held to an evangelical orthodoxy.

A Derisive Term

The name Lollard was originally a term of scorn given to the followers of John Wycliffe. It was a degrading slur that was assigned to this group sometime around the year 1385,

---

5   Diarmaid MacCulloch, *The Reformation: A History* (New York: Penguin, 2003), 35.

shortly after Wycliffe's death.[6] Though there is some uncertainty concerning the term's origin and exact meaning, the word is probably taken from a Dutch word meaning a "mumbler." "Lollard" was a derisive label of mockery used to demean these fiery gospel preachers. To unconverted ears, these men were thought to be mumbling an unintelligible message of nothing but foolish nonsense. Their message could not have been more diametrically opposed to what the Roman Catholic Church espoused.

Adding to the contempt the Lollards faced was their close connection with the controversial figure of Wycliffe himself. He had been banished from Oxford by the head of this highly esteemed university. The Lollards were labeled as Wycliffeites, because they embraced his doctrinal beliefs, which were considered false and heretical. Because Wycliffe had refuted the transubstantiation in the Mass, which was the jugular vein of Catholicism, the Lollards were assigned this controversial term by the church hierarchy of Rome.

By contrast, however, Wycliffe and the Lollards were regarded in an entirely different light by many of the common people who heard them preach. From Oxford to Gloucestershire to London, Wycliffe's spiritual insurgency against Rome was largely supported. Twenty-five percent of the population—and possibly more—are estimated to have been sympathetic to the teachings of Wycliffe and the Lollard

---

6   Carrick, *Wycliffe and the Lollards*, 200.

movement within the first fifteen years of its growth. Considering the absence of the printing press at this time, this was a remarkable expansion of their influence. The only medium for the message's spread was the spoken preached word by the Lollards, gospel tracts distributed through their preaching tours, and a limited number of portions of hand-copied Wycliffe Bibles.[7]

THE LOLLARDS BEGINNINGS (1382)

While Wycliffe was a professor at Oxford, a number of the university's scholars and students began to align themselves with his biblically grounded convictions. Among them were notable men like Nicholas Hereford, John Aston, Philip Repington, Robert Alington, and John Ashwardby. They became firebrand preachers involved in Wycliffe's contagious movement. The term Lollard was first recorded as being used by Thomas Walden and Henry Crompe, the Cistercian monk, in reference to the gospel teaching of Nicholas of Hereford and Philip Repington.[8] Their commitment to the supreme authority of the Scripture and to the exclusivity of the pure gospel was infectious and began to spread to others outside the halls of Oxford.

---

7   Ibid., 199.
8   Buddensieg, "Lollards," *The New Schaff-Herzog Encyclopedia of Religious Knowledge*, vol. VII, 15.

Preaching to Common People

A new day was dawning on the spiritual horizon of England. Buddensieg remarked, "For the first time in English history an appeal was made to the people rather than to the scholars, and dogma was superseded by the Bible, which was made the sole source of faith and practice."[9] By 1382, groups of passionate men sharing these same beliefs began to spring up in various locations around England.

Preeminent Reformation historian Merle D'Aubigne described the determined dedication of the Lollards to spread the gospel: "The 'poor priests,' as they were called, set off barefoot, a staff in their hands, clothed in a coarse robe, living on alms, and satisfied with the plainest food. . . . The people, among whom they were favourites, thronged around them. . . . They spoke with a popular eloquence that entirely won over those who listened to them."[10]

Focused upon Gospel Preaching

From the beginning of this movement, the Lollards' primary focus was upon preaching the gospel of grace through the Word of God. Wycliffe had placed the highest premium upon preaching the Scripture to people, thus amplifying the necessity of a translation of the Bible in the language of the English

---

9   Ibid.

10 J.H. Merle d'Aubigné and S.M. Houghton, *The Reformation in England*, vol. 1 (Edinburgh, Scotland: Banner of Truth Trust, 2015), 70–71.

people.[11] Anne Hudson observes of the Wycliffe Bible, "The layout seems designed for public reading: book and chapter divisions are clearly marked."[12] This was in sharp distinction from the practice of the Roman Catholic priests, who saw their chief duty as administering the sacraments, with Scripture as a mere subordinate aside.

When the priests did preach, it was done in a manner that fell woefully short of the biblical standard. Roman Catholic preaching was in Latin, and rarely from the Bible. As a result, these sermons were of little—if any—spiritual benefit to their congregants. Priests were urged by the authorities of the Roman Catholic Church to only preach four token messages a year in English, leaving the vast majority of the people in ignorance.

Preaching Unlike the Friars

What faint commitment to preaching there was in the Roman Catholic Church was carried out by the friars. This religious order was composed of men who traveled around the British Isles and Europe preaching, but not to spread the true gospel. Instead, it was to raise money for the church in Rome. They were itinerant speakers—fundraising hawkers—who traversed the countryside, speaking on the virtues of spirituality through poverty, as a means of begging for money from

---

11 Matthew Spinka, ed., *Advocates of Reform: From Wyclif to Erasmus* (Louisville, Ky.: Westminster John Knox, 2006), 31.

12 Anne Hudson, *The Premature Reformation: Wycliffite Texts and Lollard History* (Oxford, England: Clarendon, 1988), 198.

the people. These men became known as "begging friars," as they assumed pulpits to plead for contributions. They also sold religious relics for monetary gain.

Unlike their contemporaries in the Roman Catholic Church, the Lollards freely offered heaven's riches to the people, not extorting their earthly possessions. Their approach was simple—ministry began in the pulpit and reached into every facet of ministering to the people. Wycliffe believed for ministers to fulfill their calling from Christ, they must preach the Word faithfully and love the people compassionately.[13]

Expositions by the Lollards

The abuse of Roman Catholic friars only served to advance the ministry of the Lollards. While the friars announced the church's traditions and used their authority for material gain, the Lollards preached the Bible expositionally, as it was written. The influence of Wycliffe raised an indigenous force of scholars and commoners to counter the "begging friars" with a message based upon the sure truth of God's Word.[14] In the face of their opponents, the Lollards counted their condemnation to be their highest commendation, for they were charged as being preachers of the Word.

Through the Lollards, the Scripture was being read and preached in the native tongue of the English people. This brought the ire of powerful forces from London to Rome. As

13 Carrick, *Wycliffe and the Lollards*, 133.
14 Matthew Spinka, ed., *Advocates of Reform: From Wyclif to Erasmus*, 31.

John Foxe records: "The followers of Wycliffe, then called Lollards, were become extremely numerous, and the clergy were so vexed to see them increase whatever power or influence they might have to molest them in an underhanded manner, they had no authority by law to put them to death."[15]

Forerunners of the English Reformation

Tyndale scholar David Daniell noted that it was this grassroots movement of Lollard preachers that prepared the way for the coming of the English Reformation over a century later. Not even the fires of opposition, ignited by their enemies to consume them, could stop these powerful preachers of the gospel.[16]

Carrick says, "With a view to counteract the influence of the friars, Wycliffe next resolved upon a positive movement, and instituted an order of 'poor preachers'—whose vows were not in name but in reality those of poverty, chastity, and obedience."[17] The Lollards trusted in a basic truth taught by Jesus Christ—that those who humble themselves will be exalted by God. So it was that these lowly preachers were elevated to places of public influence in spreading the gospel.

Evangelists-at-Large

The Lollards traveled with the truth of Scripture in hand, moving from village to village on foot, preaching the Word

---

15 John Foxe, *Fox's Book of Martyrs*, vol. 1 (Charleston, S.C.: BiblioBazaar, 2008), 240.

16 David Daniell, *William Tyndale: A Biography* (New Haven, Conn.: Yale University Press, 1994), 31.

17 Carrick, *Wycliffe and the Lollards*, 132.

and extending the free offer of the gospel—all in Middle English. They were evangelists-at-large, known for teaching, exhorting, pleading, and warning their listeners. They went throughout England, preaching in chapels, churchyards, public streets, marketplaces, and houses. They journeyed into the countryside and cities, wherever they could gain a hearing for the Word of God. So many Lollards traveled the roads of England that it was said during their day, "You could not meet two persons on the highway but one of them a Wycliffe disciple."[18]

Lollards were men undeterred in their Christ-centered mission. They appeared to be unstoppable in their determination to spread the message of the Word of God. Because the Lollards were banished from preaching in churches, they were forced to preach outdoors in churchyards or "making a pulpit of two millstones" to preach to a gathered crowd.[19] For these foot soldiers of the cross, the proclamation of the Bible was primary—the place in which it was proclaimed was secondary. Carrick writes about these open-air preachers in earthy cathedrals: "A favourite place for their services was under the old oak-trees which from the remotest times have been characteristic of the peaceful village greens of Old England, some of these old monarchs still surviving, though much decayed, and called to this day 'Gospel Oaks.'"[20]

---

18 D'Aubigné and Houghton, *The Reformation in England*, 74.

19 Carrick, *Wycliffe and the Lollards*, 133.

20 Ibid., 175.

Equipped with Gospel Tracts

These traveling preachers were also equipped with Wycliffe's gospel tracts to distribute. Because of the tedious process of copying books by hand, few Lollard preachers possessed an entire Bible. They traveled far and wide, armed with individual sheets of these tracts or a few pages of the Bible.[21] It was only the more privileged among Wycliffe's followers who could afford a whole Bible, as the copying process was so limited, laborious, and costly.[22] They also carried with them Wycliffe's sermon outlines to follow and his pre-written sermons to preach.

This group of evangelistic expositors echoed Wycliffe's strong convictions on the sole authority of Scripture and the exclusivity of salvation in Christ alone. They held tenaciously to the truth of the free grace of God in salvation apart from human works. Initially, the Lollards were chiefly composed of Oxford scholars, who diligently studied the Word of God. They likewise included members of high social position, those immediately under the nobility known as the gentry. They were subsequently joined by many poor allies in their cause, from both rural and urban areas.

The Power of the Truth

This core group of men was wholly committed to preaching the message of salvation by grace alone and distributing gospel

---

21 Hudson, *The Premature Reformation: Wycliffite Texts and Lollard History*, 203.

22 Daniell, *William Tyndale: A Biography*, 57.

tracts. The few written resources they had were a testament to the power of their gospel message. The power lay not in the messenger, but in their Bible teaching. Carrick comments:

> Their commission was to preach the gospel, not to dispense pardons or celebrate Masses for the living or the dead, but simply clothed russet cloak, barefooted, and staff in hand, to tell the message of the cross in the towns and villages of Britain. . . . The simple Lollards, on the other hand, versed in the simple life of Christ, and profoundly impressed with a sense of His love for sinners and of the suitability of the gospel of love and peace for the world, went from town to town and from village to village preaching to the populace."[23]

After preaching the Word, these faithful evangelists would leave behind pages of Scripture or gospel tracts. It was because they were so committed to the Bible that they were so consumed with the spread of its saving truth. These faithful preachers gave their very life for what they truly believed. They were persuaded that the Word of God was an unstoppable force. Therefore, they were convinced that it must be unleashed in order for it to do its work. They understood that the written word could travel to places they could never go. These life-giving words of truth would have far-reaching effects even after they moved on to the next location.

---

23 Carrick, *Wycliffe and the Lollards*, 132–33.

Long before the English Puritans articulated this position, the Lollards believed that preaching was God's primary means of grace. They were concerned that nothing would rival the proclamation of the Scripture in the power of God to do His work. The Lollards' preaching of the biblical text was the chief vehicle for the gospel to reach England for the conversion of many souls.

Grassroots Preaching Movement

The underground movement of these traveling evangelists testifies to the importance Wycliffe had assigned to the ministry of preaching. As one strong preacher attracts other strong preachers, Wycliffe drew to himself these men who would become his successors. Only a powerful preacher such as Wycliffe could have enlisted and mobilized such an influential legion of Bible preachers. The nation of England—and the world—would never be the same.

After Wycliffe passed off the scene in 1384, the leadership of this band of preachers was assumed by the brilliant scholar Nicholas of Hereford, who had been at Wycliffe's side at Oxford. Nicholas had been assigned the primary task of translating the Old Testament into English. He was joined by influential members of the aristocratic party, as well as by common laborers throughout England. Many were enlisted through the efforts of William Swinderly, a lay preacher, and John Purvey, Wycliffe's personal secretary.

Unleashed upon England

Together, this reform-minded legion of preachers was unleashed upon England as a Bible movement more than one hundred years before the Protestant movement launched in Europe. The draw of this gospel message upon both the upper echelons and lower class workers revealed the universal call of the gospel to all people.

Though the religious climate seemed impossibly stacked against them, this marching battalion of lay preachers interpreted and heralded the Word of God independent of the established church of Rome. Lollard scholar Anne Hudson observes, "Lollardy may in a very few areas have fostered an individualism of outlook, a readiness to read the vernacular Scriptures and to interpret them independently of the ministrations from the established clergy."[24] Wycliffe had struck the match and lit the fuse for the explosive power of the gospel to set ablaze the hearts of his fellow Englishmen. The Lollards kept that torch burning.

Met with Great Opposition

As expected, the preaching of the Lollards was not without opposition. Commenting on this resistance, Lechler says:

> At the end of May, 1382, the Archbishop of Canterbury, William Courtenay, in a mandate addressed to

---

24   Hudson, *The Premature Reformation: Wycliffe Texts and Lollard History*, 61.

the Bishop of London, speaks of "certain unauthorized itinerant preachers who, as he had unhappily been compelled to learn, set forth erroneous, yea, heretical assertions in public sermons, not only in churches, but also in public squares and other profane places" and "they do this," as he adds with special emphasis, "under the guise of great holiness, but without having obtained any episcopal or papal authorization."[25]

This unauthorized activity of Lollard preaching caused great controversy. A law was passed condemning these preachers. They now could be legally arrested, tried, and sent to prison. Monks in the towns where Lollards preached would spy on their ministry and inform the authorities, seeking their imprisonment. But local believers would surround the preachers and provide them with protection from the officers. As with the first century church in Jerusalem, this opposition only advanced the greater progress of the gospel in England.

SPREADING TO EUROPE

The revival that Wycliffe began could not be contained to England, and it soon spread across the English Channel to the European continent.

---

25 Gotthard Victor Lechler and Peter Lorimer, *John Wycliffe and His English Precursors* (London: The Religious Tract Society, 1884), 190.

Wycliffe's Writings to Prague (1390)

In 1390, only six years after Wycliffe's death, his biblical teaching traveled to Bohemia (present day Czech Republic) through a student exchange program between Oxford University and the University of Prague. Students from Bohemia attended Oxford and read Wycliffe's theological works. As they learned about the gospel of salvation by grace alone through faith alone, these students were so influenced by Wycliffe's writings that they carried copies of his writings back to Prague. There, these works were read by another young student named John Hus (c. 1372–1415).

Around 1390, Hus was first introduced to Wycliffe's writings by being paid to copy them for the University of Prague library. Five copies of the complete works of Wycliffe in Hus's handwriting still remain in the Stockholm Royal Library. Through this tedious practice, Hus was directly exposed to Wycliffe's teaching and was converted by the power of the gospel. Emboldened by the truth of Scripture, Hus became an indomitable force for God. The impact of Wycliffe's writings was so great upon Hus that major portions of his writings were largely a mere restatement of what he had read and absorbed from Wycliffe. Hus became the chief instrument for the distribution of Wycliffe's teaching in Prague.

The Twelve Conclusions (1395)

Back in England, the Lollards won an unexpected reprieve late in the fourteenth century. Legislation was passed that prevented the burning of Wycliffe Bibles. The Lollards seized this opportunity for the spread of greater doctrinal clarity.[26] Knowing the vital importance of sound theology, a specific group of Lollards—members of Parliament—wrote and published a synopsis of Wycliffe's doctrinal teaching in *The Twelve Conclusions* (1395).[27] This small book was a bold manifesto that contained twelve assertions of faith. It affirmed the core doctrines of salvation that Wycliffe had preached so courageously. Likewise, it strongly refuted many papal errors, including the false teaching of transubstantiation, pilgrimages, and prayers for the dead.

This unflinching devotion to truth by the Lollards, however, was not without great cost. Because of the growing momentum of their movement, the King of England spoke out against their *Twelve Conclusions*. This denunciation by the monarch began the eventual decline of the Lollard movement as a spiritual and political force. These preachers would soon become less able to operate in the open.[28] They began to be blacklisted and forced from the influential halls of Oxford and Westminster. Nevertheless, the Lollards took their Wycliffe Bibles and continued in the work of proclaiming the truth out of the public eye.

---

26 Buddensieg, "Lollards," *The New Schaff-Herzog Encyclopedia of Religious Knowledge*, vol. VII, 16.

27 Building on the legacy of Wycliffe's own *Conclusions*, his Lollard followers would go on to produce their own version of his work.

28 Ibid.

More Wycliffe Writings to Prague (1401)

A few years later, in 1401, a Bohemian theologian and follower of John Hus, Jerome of Prague (ca. 1379–1416), returned from a trip to Oxford with more of Wycliffe's theological writings. These additional works further inspired Hus and other reformation-minded individuals in Bohemia. Subsequent leaders found Wycliffe's writings about the authentic spirituality of the true church to be insightful. Especially influential was Wycliffe's teaching that the true church consists exclusively of the total number of the elect, those predestined to eternal life.

These gospel truths birthed a reforming movement in Bohemia that would spread throughout eastern Europe for the next two centuries. Further, what Wycliffe wrote about corruption in the clergy and the false hope in purchasing indulgences resonated with Hus and many Bohemians. Hus agreed with Wycliffe, that the true church is composed exclusively of those who are predestined to grace and glory. Likewise, Hus affirmed with Wycliffe that the true head of the church is Jesus Christ alone, not the pope in Rome.

Hus preached these Wycliffe-esque truths at Bethlehem Chapel in Prague to a large congregation of 3,000 people. Hus's sermons contained lengthy citations from Wycliffe's writings. Moreover, Hus also preached in the vernacular, in the native language of his Bohemian people. Wycliffe's ministry was clearly echoed in Hus's preaching and writings. It was as though Hus was channeling the now deceased Oxford professor's fervor and courage to benefit the people who sat under his pulpit ministry.

PERSECUTION OF LOLLARDS IN ENGLAND (1401)

Meanwhile, tensions continued to rise in England. King Henry IV sought to further halt the preaching of the Lollards, while bowing to his political benefactors, such as the newly inaugurated Archbishop of Canterbury, Thomas Arundel.[29] As early as the 1380s, the anti-Lollard movement had commenced with a purge of Oxford, expelling the Lollard influence there.[30]

On the Burning of a Heretic (1401)

Perceived to be an abominable group of heretics, the Lollards nevertheless continued to work steadily into the fifteenth century. A new statute was passed by the English Parliament called *De Heretico Comburendo* (1401), meaning "On the Burning of a Heretic."

In its Preamble, this law stated its opposition against a "new sect,"[31] a reference to the Lollards. These Wycliffe-like preachers were condemned as those "who thought damnably

---

29 Ibid.

30 MacCulloch, *The Reformation: A History*, 35.

31 *Deheretico Conburendo* (1401).

of the sacraments and usurped the office of preaching."[32] This cruel statute empowered the bishops of England to initiate the arrest, examination, imprisonment, and martyrdom of all supposed "heretics" who contradicted the teaching of Rome.

This legislation made preaching the true gospel a crime worthy of death. Those found guilty were turned over to the government authorities and promptly burned at the stake. This grisly execution was to take place "in a high place,"[33] so that the populace would witness it. The intent was to strike fear into the hearts of those who would follow this new teaching. Their ruthless legislation was aimed at halting the building momentum of the Lollard movement—one that increasingly threatened the corrupt power of the Roman Catholic Church over the people of England.

The Burning of William Sawtrey (1401)

The implementation of this vicious purge was as swift as it was brutal. Only one month from the passing of the new law, the burning stake consumed its first Lollard, a man named William Sawtrey. Having been arrested for charges of heresy on multiple occasions prior to his death, Sawtrey had wavered on his confession and recanted. But when arrested again, this time he was ready to suffer for the truth of Scripture. The Roman Catholic priest-turned-Lollard was charged with eight

32 Ibid.
33 Ibid.

crimes of heresy and "relapse" on February 26, 1401, at St. Paul's Cathedral in London.[34]

Each charge brought against Sawtrey deepened his belief in the exclusive authority of Scripture, which resounded with the voice of his predecessor, John Wycliffe. After being convicted by a gathering of church authorities, Sawtrey was stripped of his priestly ordination and ministry. He was turned over to the civil authorities of England and burned at the stake at Smithfield in London, where vast numbers of faithful English martyrs would pass to glory in the centuries to come.[35] The blood of Lollard martyrs was now plowing the soil for the seeds of the gospel to be later sown in the coming Reformation.

ALL ENGLISH BIBLES BANNED (1408)

In addition to their preaching, the Lollards were perceived to be a threat to the English nation because of their work in distributing copies of the Wycliffe Bible as they traveled to preach. At this tense time, even owning a Wycliffe Bible was a crime punishable by death at the stake. But the Lollards would not be intimidated. Rather than halting this gospel movement, this resistance caused its members to grow stronger in their resolve to preach the saving message of Jesus Christ.

---

34 "William Sawtrey," *The Reformation*, accessed May 22, 2020, https://www.the reformation.info/sawtrey/.

35 Margery Kempe, *The Book of Margery Kempe*, trans. Barry Windeatt (United Kingdom: Penguin, 2005), 17.

The Constitutions of Oxford (1408)

Further opposition was taken against the Wycliffite preachers in 1408 when Thomas Arundell, the archbishop of Canterbury, presided over a synod in Oxford that passed "The Constitutions of Oxford." These declarations strictly forbade any translation of the Bible into English and prohibited any use of a Wycliffe Bible, whether for private reading or public preaching. This was another attempt to intimidate the Lollards and halt their preaching. As stated previously, the "Constitutions" legislated control over the theological education in the colleges at the University of Oxford. As it relates to Wycliffe's Bible, the "Constitutions" read as follows: "It is a dangerous thing . . . to translate the text of the Holy Scripture out of one tongue into another, for in the translation the same sense is not always easily kept. . . . We therefore decree and ordain, that no man hereafter, by his own authority translate any text of the Scripture into English or any other tongue."[36]

Despite the anti-Wycliffe verdicts of this synod at Oxford, the Lollards remained unwavering in their determination to transmit the witness of the truths of the Word of God.

---

36 Thomas Arundel's *Constitutions of Oxford, Seventh Condemnation*, quoted in Kristy Campbell, "Vernacular *Auctoritas* in Late Medieval England: Writing after the Constitutions," in *Author, Reader, Book: Medieval Authorship in Theory and Practice*, eds. Stephen Partridge and Erik Kwakkel (Toronto: University of Toronto Press, 2012), 194.

The Mirror Of Jesus Christ (1410)

In 1410, twenty-six years after Wycliffe's death, the wickedness of the church was further institutionalized by his archnemesis Thomas Arundel. At that time, Arundel licensed a work by Nicholas Love entitled *The Mirror of the Blessed Life of Jesus Christ* as a response to the Lollard Bible and the preaching of Wycliffe's followers. *The Mirror* was intended to serve as a translation of the Bible that combined "devotional" material rooted in the practice of Roman Catholic doctrine and tinged with aberrant interpretations and mysticism.

Arundel said in his licensure of this book that it was, "[for] the edification of the faithful and the confutation of heretics or Lollards."[37] The goal of Love's work was aimed at stopping the spread of Wycliffe's teaching. It was a work rooted not in the Word of God, but in the deeply ingrained tradition of the church.

John Oldcastle Imprisoned (1413, 1414)

By the 1410s, the Oxford scholars, who first stood with Wycliffe when the Lollard movement began, started to pass on to heaven. In this transition period, the movement became more layman-oriented. The leadership of the Lollards was assumed by Sir John Oldcastle, an English soldier, member of Parliament, and prominent landowner. His status as an influential figure was enhanced by his marriage to the daughter

---

37 Kantik Ghosh, *Power, Prestige, and Authority in Medieval Manuscripts and Texts*, ed. Felicity Riddy (United Kingdom: Boydell & Brewer, 2000), 18.

of the baron of Cobham.[38] Oldcastle urged these itinerant evangelists to continue their mission by boldly preaching the gospel. Though not a preacher himself, Oldcastle gave safe harbor and material aid to these followers of Wycliffe's legacy.

Like many other leaders in the movement, Oldcastle was convicted of "Wycliffe heresy," imprisoned, and condemned as a heretic on September 23, 1413. In an attempt to crush the Lollard movement, the authorities granted him a period of forty days to reconsider and recant, and thus effectively terminate the Lollard movement by his capitulation. During this time, however, he escaped from the Tower of London and unwisely conspired an attempt to capture King Henry V in the Christmas season of that year, during his stay at Eltham. The first attempt having failed, a second attempt was planned in London in early 1414, but was foiled when the king was apprised of the secret meeting taking place on January 12 of that year. Oldcastle escaped again and spent the next three years as an outlaw and fugitive from the crown.

This foiled coup cost the Lollards much needed credibility with the political establishment and wealthy aristocrats. M. Creighton noted that Oldcastle "seems to have been a man of genuine piety, but without much discretion."[39] From this point forward, this dissenting movement would primarily be comprised of common people outside the circles of

---

38 M. Creighton, "Lollards," *The New Schaff-Herzog Encyclopedia of Religious Knowledge*, vol. II (New York: Funk & Wagnalls, 1883), 1339.

39 Ibid.

established power in England. This lack of influential leadership forced the Lollards underground, where they operated mainly in London and southern England.

The Lantern Of Light (1415)

Despite this growing opposition, the Lollards continued to fight for the authority of the Word of God to establish the church's worship and ministry. In their publication *The Lantern of Light,* these stalwart men challenged any claim to authority outside of Scripture alone. They wrote: "Here some object that the gospel is not of authority but in as much as the church has authorized it and canonized it, for they say that no man knows such words to be the gospel, but as the church has determined in her determination. This conclusion seems to smack of heresy."[40]

The Lollards would not tolerate the idea of lowering the divinely-inspired Word of God to any ecclesiastical hierarchy. They would not yield the high ground of its clear teaching to the fallible whims of men. The pontifications of the established church of Rome, they contended, were the cause of its internal weaknesses. Only a revival in the preaching of God's word, they believed, would reform the church and restore it to spiritual vitality.

---

40 Ibid.

THE RAGING FIRES OF PERSECUTION

Rather than the resistance to Wycliffe's theology subsiding, the raging fires of persecution only increased. The worst was yet to come. Nevertheless, God would bring much good from it as this escalating of persecution would ultimately be the pathway to prepare for the coming of the Reformation in the sixteenth century.

The Condemning of Wycliffe (1415)

From 1414 to 1418, the Council of Constance met in modern-day Germany, as an ecumenical council of the Roman Catholic Church, to deliberate over many issues. In 1415, thirty-one years after Wycliffe died, the Council of Constance condemned him on 260 counts of heresy. The Council ordered that Wycliffe's writings be burned and that his bones be exhumed and taken out of consecrated ground in the churchyard where he was buried.

But Wycliffe's bones were more easily destroyed than his lasting influence. Despite the church's opposition to Wycliffe's Bible, its impact was deeply felt throughout England and pervasive even into the European continent. This resistance against an English Bible and the persecution it brought only intensified over the next century.

The Burning of Hus (1415)

The Council of Constance also summoned John Hus, the Prague preacher, to appear in order to defend his Wycliffe-like teaching. Hus had been promised safe passage, but was betrayed by the authorities. He was tried, found guilty, and turned over to the civil authorities in Bohemia to be burned at the stake. The charge read: "This holy synod of Constance, seeing that God's church has nothing more that it can do, relinquishes John Hus to the judgment of the secular authority (July 6, 1415)."[41]

The Burning of Jerome (1415)

Jerome of Prague (1379–1416), who had brought Wycliffe's writings to Prague, was also summoned to appear before the Council. Jerome, a scholastic philosopher, theologian, and reformer, was known to be one of Hus' chief supporters and followers. He was arrested, judged, condemned of heresy, and turned over to the same secular authorities in Prague to be burned at the stake. His only crime was spreading the doctrines taught by Wycliffe.

John Oldcastle Martyred (1417)

Despite his earlier political indiscretions in trying to kidnap the king, Oldcastle remained faithful to the cause of Christ. His life demonstrates the high cost of faithfulness to the gospel and the Word of God. Though history may record his demise as the result of his political insurrection, it must be remembered that the heart of his actions were

---

41 Council of Constance, "Council of Constance 1414–18," Papal Encyclicals Online, accessed July 23, 2020, https://www.papalencyclicals.net/councils/ecum16.htm.

driven by a commitment to right doctrine and the work of John Wycliffe.

In late 1417, Oldcastle's hiding place in Wales was discovered and he was finally apprehended after being seriously wounded in the subsequent pursuit. He was taken to London and promptly condemned to death for his actions as both a traitor, and a Lollard. On that same day, December 14, 1417, he was drawn, hanged, and then burned while hanging for his offenses. This violent martyrdom was a further repudiation of Wycliffe and his biblical convictions. Moreover, it was a devastating blow that forced the Lollard movement even deeper underground.

Wycliffe's Ashes Scattered (1428)

Finally, in 1428, the pope ordered that Wycliffe's remains should be dug up and burned, and his ashes scattered into the Swift River.

One historian notes that the influence of Wycliffe could not be contained: "They burnt his bones to ashes and cast them into the Swift, a neighboring brook running hard by. Thus the brook has conveyed his ashes into the Avon; Avon into Severn; Severn into the narrow seas; and they into the main ocean. And thus the ashes of Wycliffe are the emblem of his doctrine which now is dispersed the world over."[42]

Because Wycliffe's impact was felt throughout England

---

42   Schaff and Schaff, *History of the Christian Church*, vol. VI, 325.

and the European continent, his further condemnation from his enemies had unwittingly constructed a bridge that would extend his influence for generations to come.

Lollards Pushed Underground (1450)

The Lollards' powerful effect as agents of change in England waned greatly after 1450 when they ceased to produce more meaningful writings. In contrast to the Reformation in the next century, the Lollards' influence became relatively obscured beyond their own lifetimes. This dwindling effect was in large part because they lacked the tools of communication, primarily the printing press. Further, they made no contribution to popular music and the legacy of hymn-writing to keep their teachings in circulation.[43] In 1519, seven Lollards were burned at the stake for the "dangerous" act of simply teaching their children the Lord's Prayer in English. The tensions between the established church and the true church continued to escalate to a fever pitch.

FROM WYCLIFFE TO THE REFORMERS

Though the Lollard movement was pushed underground by the persecution it faced, the Bible-centered influence of Wycliffe continued to move forward. What began in England with Wycliffe and the Lollards soon spread to Bohemia with

---

43 MacCulloch, *The Reformation: A History*, 36.

John Hus, and it eventually came to Germany with Martin Luther. Through Luther's writings, this Bible movement would return back to England and capture the life of William Tyndale.

Martin Luther Emerges (1519)

These sparks of truth ignited the Reformation as it was passed to John Hus upon reading Wycliffe, and subsequently to Martin Luther (1483–1546). Such was the influence of Wycliffe upon Luther, which emboldened the German Reformer to take his stand upon the Word of God—even if he would have to stand alone. Luther demonstrated his Wycliffe-like resolve in the great Leipzig Disputation (1519) with Johann Eck by stating, "It is of little consequence to me whether these things were said by Wycliffe or by Hus . . . they are truth."[44]

When Luther responded to Erasmus with his magnum opus, *The Bondage of the Will*, he made mention that only Wycliffe stood with him, seemingly against the entire world. Luther boldly declared:

> You are much influenced (you tell us) by the great array of learned men, objects of many centuries' unanimous acclaim, some of them expert Biblical scholars, some of them great saints, some martyrs, many renowned for miracles, plus the theologians of more recent times

---

44 Martin Luther quoted in J.H. Merle D'Aubigne, *History of the Reformation of the Sixteenth Century*, vol. II (1875; repr., Sprinkle, 2003), 58.

and an abundance of schools, councils, bishops and popes beside. In short (you say) there stands on your side scholarship, ability, numbers, dignity, distinction, courage, holiness, miracles and what not else, while on my side there is just Wycliffe.[45]

The Tyndale Bible (1526, 1533–1534, 1535)

The Wycliffe Bible was the only English Bible that a select few would possess until 1526 with the appearance of a new translation by William Tyndale. This was followed by two revised editions of the New Testament and the Pentateuch (1530), Jonah (1531), and the Historical Books (1535) in the Old Testament. This translation would be done from the Greek and Hebrew with which it was originally written.

A Perpetual Legacy

A century and a half after Wycliffe's death, he was still being attacked for his work in translating the Bible into the language of the English people. His name continued to be slandered by the religious establishment for his convictions. His supposed wrongdoing was recovering the true gospel, exposing heresy, and translating the Bible into his native tongue.

By passing the torch to the Lollards, Wycliffe created a groundswell movement that could not be stopped. The commitment of Wycliffe to the Bible was handed down to the

---

45 Martin Luther, *The Bondage of the Will*, trans. J.I. Packer and O.R. Johnston (Grand Rapids, Mich.: Revell, 1957), 109.

Reformers, and their influence carries over to our own generation. The Word of God must continue to be translated into the languages of all peoples around the world. The need has never been greater than in this present hour for the Scripture to be accessible to the people groups of the world.

May the legacy of John Wycliffe be extended to all peoples around the globe. A new generation of Bible believers must not rest until the work of Wycliffe is carried out in proclaiming the truth of the Scripture to all nations.

We Want Again
Wycliffes

What can we learn from the life and ministry of John Wycliffe?

More than anything else, we are reminded yet again of the supreme importance of the Word of God in the Christian life. We see the fundamental truth that there is no entrance into the kingdom of God apart from knowing and believing the saving message of the Bible. Further, we observe that there is no advancement in spiritual growth into Christlikeness apart from the Scripture. Without the Word of God, no one can be saved. And no one can be sanctified.

This truth should be abundantly clear through being introduced to the life mission of Wycliffe. He was a man who was willing to pay any price to bring the Word of God to the people of his country. He was willing to risk his personal livelihood and reputation to place into the hands of his fellow

Englishmen a Bible they could read and understand. The sacrifices that Wycliffe made were enormous, as he died in the midst of producing an English Bible.

We have dire need of brave men and women like this today—those who are willing to go to great lengths to spread the message of God's Word. In this present hour, the challenges to be a Christian and follow Christ continue to escalate. We are living in a world that is growing increasingly intolerant toward the exclusive truth claims of the Bible. In light of this ongoing opposition, we have a need for Wycliffes to step to the forefront as never before.

My desire is that through the pages of this book, you have been reawakened to the primary importance of the Word of God for all of life. My intent is that you would see in the life of John Wycliffe, this extraordinary pre-Reformer, the kind of unrelenting commitment that is required to bring about a thorough Reformation yet again.

In our present day, the need has never been greater for a new generation of preachers to rise up to preach the Word. This modern hour demands that strong Christians proclaim the strong message of the saving gospel of God. May a new army of biblical expositors hold high the torch of truth in this dark night of history and usher in a new day for the church, as Wycliffe and the Lollards so powerfully displayed.

I call you to examine your own life and ask the Lord what part He would have you play in spreading the Word of God to others. Are you a mother or father? Teach your children the

Bible. Are you a grandparent? Instruct your grandchildren in the Scripture. Where has God placed you vocationally? Do you work in the business community? Do you serve in the medical field? Do you teach in a school? Take the Word of God into that marketplace. What is the ministry into which God has called you? Bring the Bible into that arena. Are you a pastor? Preach the Word.

As you have read about the life of John Wycliffe in this book, may it serve as a strong motivation for you to live a fruitful life that is rooted and grounded in the fertile soil of Scripture. We want—again—Wycliffes, those who will impact this world with the sacred truths of God's Word.

May you be that man or woman whose life is fully invested in taking the message of the Bible into this troubled world. Wherever God will lead you, whether across the street or around the globe, may you, like Wycliffe, lead a life full of Bible conviction.

INDEX

ABOUT THE AUTHOR

D r. Steven J. Lawson is president and founder of OnePassion, a ministry designed to equip biblical expositors to bring about a new reformation in the church. Dr. Lawson is teacher for The Institute for Expository Preaching in cities around the world. He is a teaching fellow for Ligonier Ministries and professor of preaching at The Master's Seminary, where he is dean of the doctor of ministry program. He also serves as a member of the board at both Ligonier and The Master's Seminary. In addition, he is the executive editor for *Expositor Magazine*.

Dr. Lawson served as a pastor for thirty-four years in Arkansas and Alabama. Most recently, he was senior pastor of Christ Fellowship Baptist Church in Mobile, Ala. He is a graduate of Texas Tech University (B.B.A.), Dallas Theological Seminary (Th.M.), and Reformed Theological Seminary (D.Min.).

Dr. Lawson is the author of more than two dozen books, including *New Life in Christ*, *The Moment of Truth*, *The Kind of Preaching God Blesses*, *The Heroic Boldness of Martin Luther*, *The Gospel Focus of Charles Spurgeon*, *Foundations of Grace*, *Pillars of Grace*, *Famine in the Land*, verse-by-verse commentaries on Psalms and Job for the Holman Old Testament Commentary series, and *Philippians for You* in the God's Word for You series. He also serves as editor of the Long Line of Godly Men Profiles series with Ligonier Ministries.

Dr. Lawson's books have been translated into many languages, including Russian, Italian, Portuguese, Spanish, German, Albanian, Korean, and Indonesian. He has contributed articles to magazines and theological journals including *Tabletalk*, *Banner of Truth*, *The Master's Seminary Journal*, *The Southern Baptist Journal of Theology*, *Bibliotheca Sacra*, *Decision*, and *Discipleship Journal*.